On a Discourse that Might not Be a Semblance

Jacques Lacan

On a Discourse that Might not Be a Semblance

The Seminar of Jacques Lacan
Book XVIII

Edited by Jacques-Alain Miller

Translated by Bruce Fink

polity

Originally published in French as *Le Séminaire. Livre XVIII. D'un discours qui ne serait pas du semblant* © Éditions du Seuil, 2006

This English translation © Polity Press, 2025

Polity Press
65 Bridge Street
Cambridge CB2 1UR, UK

Polity Press
111 River Street
Hoboken, NJ 07030, USA

ISBN-13: 978-1-5095-1010-8 – hardback

A catalogue record for this book is available from the British Library.

Library of Congress Control Number: 2024936758

Typeset in 10.5 on 12 pt Times NR MT
by Cheshire Typesetting Ltd, Cuddington, Cheshire
Printed and bound in Great Britain by CPI Group (UK) Ltd, Croydon

The publisher has used its best endeavours to ensure that the URLs for external websites referred to in this book are correct and active at the time of going to press. However, the publisher has no responsibility for the websites and can make no guarantee that a site will remain live or that the content is or will remain appropriate.

Every effort has been made to trace all copyright holders, but if any have been overlooked the publisher will be pleased to include any necessary credits in any subsequent reprint or edition.

For further information on Polity, visit our website:
politybooks.com

Contents

Translator's Note

Numbers found in the margins here correspond to the pagination of the 2006 French edition of Lacan's Seminar XVIII, *D'un discours qui ne serait pas du semblant*, edited by Jacques-Alain Miller and published by Éditions du Seuil in Paris. All references here to Lacan's Écrits (Paris: Seuil, 1966) are to the pagination of *Écrits: The First Complete Edition in English* (New York & London: W. W. Norton & Co., 2006). When I refer to Lacan's Seminars, I provide the pagination of the English editions, when they exist; when they do not, I give the page number(s) in the French editions. All the extant Seminars except Seminar VI were published in French by Éditions du Seuil in Paris. Seminar VI was published by La Martinière/Le Champ freudien. Seminars that have yet to be published in French are indicated by volume number and date of class. References to Freud's work here are always to *The Standard Edition of the Complete Psychological Works of Sigmund Freud* (twenty-four volumes) published in London by Hogarth Press, abbreviated here as SE, followed by the volume number and page(s). Words followed by an asterisk (*) are found in English in the original. Text in square brackets has been added by the translator.

I wish to thank Héloïse Fink for help with the French, Tao Zhang and Zhuoxuan Li for help with the Chinese, Elizabeth Oyler for help with Lacan's comments on Japanese and with Chinese characters, and Dany Nobus for help with Chapter VII.

Figures

I

INTRODUCING THE TITLE
OF THE SEMINAR

> *D'un discours qui ne serait pas du semblant*
> On a Discourse That Might Not Be a Semblance

[On the blackboard]

"On a discourse" – it's not mine.

I believe I managed to sufficiently impress upon you last year what we must understand by the term "discourse." Let me recall to mind here the master's discourse and its four positions, as I call them, and the quarter turns of its terms in a structure that is reduced to being tetrahedral. I left it to whoever wanted to do so to explain what justifies these shifts, which could have been more varied. I reduced them to four. I will perhaps indicate to you this year why these four [out of twenty-four] should be granted priority, if no one else does so.

I only referred to them owing to my aim, which was stated in the title of last year's Seminar: *L'Envers de la psychanalyse* [The Other Side (or: the Reverse or Flip Side) of Psychoanalysis]. The master's discourse is not the flip side of psychoanalysis; it is where the characteristic twist, as I will call it, of psychoanalytic discourse is demonstrated.

For you are aware of the importance that was immediately attributed to Freud's theory of double inscription, and the emphasis that was placed on it. It raises the question of a front and a back. But I tried to highlight for you the possibility of a double inscription, on the front and back, without any edge being crossed.

Such is the structure, which has long been familiar to us, that goes by the name of the Möbius strip. All I had to do was make use of it.

1

These positions and terms designate the fact that what discourse is, strictly speaking, can in no wise be located on the basis of a subject, even if discourse determines the subject.

Therein perhaps lies the ambiguity of the way I introduced what I thought I had to convey within psychoanalytic discourse.

Recall the terms I used, at the time at which I entitled a certain paper "Function and Field of Speech and Language in Psychoanalysis." "Intersubjectivity," I wrote at the time – and Lord knows what false leads enunciating terms like that can give rise to. Please excuse me for having had to start by doing so. I could but be met with misunderstanding. "Inter," sure. Indeed, only what came afterward allowed me to enunciate it in the form of an "intersignifierness" [*intersignifiance*], giving rise to subjectivity, the signifier being what represents a subject to another signifier, where the subject is not. Where the subject is represented, he is absent. That is why he finds himself divided in this way, being represented all the same.

It is not simply that discourse can thus no longer be judged merely in light of its unconscious mainspring. It can no longer be stated as something other than what is articulated on the basis of a structure in which the subject turns out to be irreducibly alienated somewhere.

Hence my introductory statement: "On a discourse" – I'll stop there – "it's not mine." I am beginning my discussion of "a discourse that would (like) not (to) be based on semblance" this year with the statement that discourse cannot be the discourse of any specific person, but is instead based on a structure, and with the accent given to it by the distribution and slippage of certain of its terms.

To those of you who were not present last year to hear these remarks, which are preliminary, let me indicate that some of them can be found in written form in issue number 2/3 of the journal *Scilicet*, which came out over a month ago already.

Owing to the fact that it contains writing, *Scilicet* 2/3 is a discursive event, if not an advent. It is so, first of all, because psychoanalytic discourse, whose instrument I happen to be – and we can't overlook the fact that this discourse necessitates your crowded presence here, in other words, that you be here and in the precise form of something odd that makes news [or: makes you squeeze in here, *fait la presse*], owing, surely, let us say, to the impact of our history – renews the question of the status of discourse qua master's discourse. One can but wonder when we pronounce its name [*le dénommer*]. Don't immediately jump to the word "revolution." But it is clear that we must discern the status of what, in short, allows me to propose such remarks – namely, the formulation "On a discourse that might not be a semblance" [or: "On a discourse that would (like) not (to) be based on semblance"].

Two things should be noted about the most recent issue of *Scilicet*.

The first is that I actually put last year's discourse to the test – except that I included something extra – in a configuration that is specifically characterized by the absence of what I called your crowded presence. To fully highlight what this presence signifies, I will qualify it as *plus-de-jouir pressé* [crowded, rushed, freshly squeezed, or extracted surplus jouissance].

It is on the basis of this exact figure that we can gauge whether it goes beyond a certain discomfort, as they say, regarding too much semblance in the discourse in which you are inscribed: university [or: academic] discourse. It is easy to expose it as tantamount to discomfort with a neutrality, for example, that this discourse cannot claim to maintain, either on the basis of a competitive selection – when what is involved are signs that are addressed solely to those in the know – or on the basis of a subject's education, when something entirely different is at stake. What would it take to go beyond this discomfort with semblance and be able to hope for something that allows us to leave that behind? The only thing that allows us to do so is positing that a certain mode of rigor in the advancement of analytic discourse splits [or: breaks up (or interrupts), *clive*] – in a dominant position in this discourse – the triage of these globules of surplus jouissance owing to which you find yourselves caught up in university discourse.

What constitutes the originality of this teaching, and thus explains what you contribute to it by crowding in here – this is not new, as I've already said it, but no one pays it any heed – is that someone, on the basis of analytic discourse, is situating himself in the position of an analysand with respect to you. When I spoke on the radio [see "Radiophonie" in *Scilicet* 2/3], I put my teaching to the test of the absence of your presence, of the space into which you crowd, canceled out and replaced by the pure "It exists" of the intersignifierness I spoke about earlier, so that the subject flickers [*vacille*] there. I am simply changing tack toward something the possible import of which the future will tell.

Something else should be noted about what I called this discursive event or advent. As a certain number of you already know, people write what is printed in *Scilicet* without signing their names to it. What does that mean? It means that each of the names found in a column on the last page of the three issues that make up a year can be permutated with each of the others, asserting thereby that no discourse has a single author. That is a wager. And it makes quite a statement. The future will show whether in five or six years, all the journals – all the good journals, I mean – will do the same thing. It is a wager. We'll see.

In what I say, I do not try to leave behind what is sensed or felt in my statements to emphasize, and stick to, discourse as artifactual [*l'artefact du discours*]. This is, of course, to say – it's the least one can say – that in so doing, it is out of the question that I claim to encompass everything. What I say cannot constitute a system, and in this regard, it is not a philosophy. It is clear to anyone who considers the angle from which psychoanalysis allows us to revamp the status of discourse that this implies that we operate, as it were, in a disuniverse. This is not the same thing as the diverse. Yet I wouldn't object to this "diverse" – and not only owing to what it implies by way of diversity, but by way of diversion, too.

It is also very clear that I do not talk about everything [or: the whole, *tout*]. Furthermore, what I say impedes our talking about the "whole." This is obvious every day. The fact that I don't say everything even regarding what I state is another matter; as I've already said, it owes to the fact that truth can only be half-told.

In short, this discourse – which confines itself to acting in the artifactual – is thus merely an extension of the analyst's position, insofar as it is defined by placing the weight of its surplus jouissance in a certain place. This is nevertheless a position I cannot occupy here, precisely because I am not in the position of an analyst here. As I said earlier, you here in the crowd [*presse*] would be in that position, if you had the knowledge that goes with it. That said, what can be the import of what I am stating with this "On a discourse that might not be a semblance" [or: "On a discourse that would (like) not (to) be based on semblance"]?

This can be stated from my position, and as a function of what I stated before. In any case, it is a fact that I am stating it. Let me point out that is also a fact *because* I am stating it. You might see nothing in this – in other words, think that there is nothing here beyond the fact that I am stating it. However, if I have characterized discourse as artifactual, it is because, as regards discourse, whatever is done, so to speak, is done only by speaking [or: there are facts only owing to the fact of speaking them, *il n'y a de fait que du fait de le dire*]. A stated fact owes entirely to discourse. This is what I am designating with the term "artifact," and it is, of course, what must be eliminated.

13   Indeed, if I speak about what is artifactual, it is not to give rise to the idea of something that would (like to) be different – in other words, natural. You would be wrong to go down that path, because you will never work your way out of the quandaries you encounter

there. The question is not "Is it or isn't it discourse?" but rather "It is said or it is not said."

I am beginning from what is said in a discourse, whose artifactual nature is presumed to suffice for you to be here.

I am cutting myself off here, for I am not adding for you to be here "in the form of crowded surplus jouissance."

I said "cutting" because it is unclear whether it is as *already* crowded [or: freshly squeezed (or rushed or extracted)] surplus jouissance that my discourse brings you together. It is not cut and dried [*tranché*], regardless of what this one or that one may think, that it is this discourse – the one constituted by the series of statements I make to you – that puts you in this position.

2

What does "*du semblant*" [semblance, or on the basis of (mere) semblance] mean in my title this year?

If it means, for example, *Du semblant de discours* [(based on) a semblance of discourse], that would be the position known as "logical positivism" where one puts a signified to the test of something that decisively says [or: decides, *tranche*] yes or no. Whatever cannot be put to that test is defined as having no meaning at all.

The logical positivists believe they can thereby eliminate a certain number of questions characterized as metaphysical. I am certainly not attached to such questions, but I would point out that logical positivism is untenable, at least on the basis of psychoanalytic experience.

If psychoanalytic experience happens to derive its claim to nobility from the Oedipal myth, it is because it preserves the peremptoriness [*tranchant*] of the oracle's enunciation, and, I would go even further, because interpretation always remains at that level. For an interpretation is only rendered true by what it gives rise to, just like an oracle's pronouncements. Interpretation does not involve putting truth to the test, leading to [*se trancherait*] a simple yes or no; it in fact *unleashes* the truth. It is true only inasmuch as it is truly followed by effects [or: corroborated, *suivie*].

We shall see later that the very schemas of logical implication, in its most classical form, require the backdrop of the veridical insofar as it belongs to speech, even if it is, strictly speaking, meaning- 14
less. The shift from a time when truth is determined on the basis of [*se tranche de*] its unleashing alone to a logic that attempts to give body to this truth, is the precise moment at which discourse, qua representative of representation [*Vorstellungsrepräsentanz*], is

disqualified. But if it can be disqualified, it is because it is always already disqualified somewhere. This is what is known as repression. It is no longer a representation that it represents; rather, the corroborative discourse that follows is characterized as a truth effect [*c'est cette suite de discours qui se caractérise comme effet de vérité*].

A truth effect is not mere semblance [or: based on semblance, *du semblant*]. The Oedipus complex is there to teach us that, if you will, real blood [or: red blood, *sang rouge*] is spilled. Yet the spilling of blood does not refute semblance; it colors it, renders it re-semblant, and propagates it. A little sawdust to soak up the blood and the whole circus begins anew. This is why the question of a discourse that might not be a semblance [or: would (like) not (to) be based on semblance] can be elevated to the level of an artifact of the structure of discourse [or: of the artifactual structure of discourse, *l'artefact de la structure du discours*]. In the meantime, there is no semblance of discourse, there is no metalanguage by which to evaluate it, there is no Other of the Other, and there is no truth about truth.

I once got a kick out of making truth speak [*Écrits*, p. 340]. What can be truer than the enunciation "I am lying?" Where, I ask, is the paradox? The classical quibbling involving the term "paradox" becomes weighty only if you write "I am lying" on a piece of paper. Everyone senses that there is nothing truer that can be said at times than to say "I am lying." It is even quite certainly the only truth that does not occasionally crumble [*brisé*]. Who doesn't realize that by saying "I am not lying," one is absolutely not safe from saying something false? What does this mean? Who is speaking when the truth at issue – the truth about which I said that it speaks "I," the truth that is enunciated qua oracle – speaks? This semblance is the signifier itself.

I use the signifier in a way that bothers linguists. There was one who wrote a few lines designed to warn people that Ferdinand de Saussure obviously had no idea what he was talking about. How do we know? Ferdinand de Saussure did what I do: he didn't say everything. The proof is that people found things in his papers that he never discussed in his course in general linguistics.

People think that the signifier is a nice little thing that is domesticated by structuralism – people think that the signifier is the Other qua Other, the battery of signifiers, and everything I explain.

It's divine, naturally, because I am an idealist at times.

3

"Artifact," I said to begin with.

It is absolutely clear that artifacts are, naturally, our daily fare; we find them everywhere, within arm's reach at every turn. If there is a discourse that can be maintained, or that is, in any case, maintained, that is known as the discourse of science, it is perhaps worth recalling that it began quite specifically by considering semblances.

What is the starting point of scientific thought, historically speaking? The observation of the heavenly bodies. And which ones, if not constellations – in other words, the most typical semblance. What do the first steps of modern physics revolve around at the outset? Not around the elements, as people think, for the elements – the four of them, and even if you add the fifth, quintessence – are already discourse, philosophical discourse, and how! The first steps of modern physics revolve around meteors.

Descartes wrote a "Treatise on Meteors." The decisive step, or, rather, one of the decisive steps, concerns the theory of rainbows. In talking about meteors [atmospheric phenomena], I am referring to things that are defined as sheer semblance. No one, even among the most primitive peoples, ever believed that a rainbow was something that was there, curved and standing up in the sky. Rainbows were investigated as meteors.

The most typical and earliest meteor – the one that is indubitably linked to the very structure of discourse – is thunder. There was nothing fanciful in the fact that I ended my "Rome Discourse" by evoking thunder. There is no Name-of-the-Father that is tenable without thunder, and everyone knows that it is a sign, even if we don't know what it is a sign of. It is the very picture of semblance.

This is why there is no such thing as a semblance of discourse [or: discursive semblance (or discourse qua semblance), *semblant de discours*]. All that is discourse can but present itself as semblance, and nothing is constructed there that isn't based on what is known as the signifier. In the light in which I am presenting it today, the signifier is identical to the very status of semblance.

"On a discourse that might not be a semblance" [or: "On a discourse that would (like) not (to) be based on semblance"]. For that to be enunciated, it is necessary, thus, that the "based on (a) semblance" not be completable in any way by referring to "discourse" [as in "based on a semblance of discourse"]. Something else is at stake – the referent no doubt. But sit tight a minute. This referent is probably not automatically the object, because what this means is precisely that the referent is what shifts around. The semblance in which discourse is identical to itself is a level of the term "semblance" – it is semblance in nature.

It is no accident that I reminded you that no discourse that mentions nature has ever done anything but begin from semblance in nature. For nature is full of it. I'm not talking about animal nature, where it is obvious that it abounds plentifully. This is even what makes it such that there are silly geese who believe that all of animal nature, from the fish to the birds, sings the praises of God. That is self-evident. Every time they open something, whether a mouth or an operculum, it is blatant semblance. Nothing necessitates these gaps.

We are entering here into something whose efficacy has not been determined, for the simple reason that we don't know how it happened that an accumulation of signifiers occurred, as it were. For signifiers, as I am telling you, are scattered about the world; we find them by the bucketful in nature. In order for language to be born – it is already quite something to raise the question – it was necessary that something be established somewhere that I already indicated to you regarding Pascal's wager, which is that we don't remember it. What is annoying about presuming this is that it already assumes the functioning of language, because it involves the unconscious. The unconscious and its workings mean that, among the numerous signifiers that circulate in the world, there is going to be a fragmented body, too.

There are, nevertheless, things one can view as already existing in a certain functioning, without us being required to consider the accumulation of signifiers. These are matters of turf [or: turf wars].

If your signifier "right arm" [or: straight arm (or right-hand man), *bras droit*] goes to pick something in your neighbor's yard – such things happen all the time – your neighbor naturally grabs your signifier "right arm" and chucks it back over the fence. That is what you curiously enough call "projection," isn't it? It is a way of getting along [or: being understood, *s'entendre*]. That should be our starting point. If your right arm were not completely occupied with picking apples from your neighbor's tree, for example, if it had stayed still, your neighbor might well have adored it. This is the origin of the master signifier – a straight arm, the scepter.

The master signifier needs nothing more to get started, at the outset. But, unfortunately, a little more is required. A little more and you get the scepter. The thing immediately materializes as a signifier. But according to all the evidence we have about it, the historical process turns out to be a bit more complicated.

It is clear that the little parable with which I began, that of an arm that is chucked back from one territory into another, is still an unsatisfying schema. It needn't be *your* arm that comes back to you, because signifiers are not individual – we don't know to whom each one belongs. So you see, we are entering here into another kind of early game regarding the function of chance and that of myths.

We should try to understand a little bit about what happened. Imagine a world. In this case, let us imagine a schema or a medium that is divided into a certain number of territorial cells. After all, in this process of expulsion – which you call "projection," although we don't know why, unless it is thrown to you like a projectile, of course – you may receive not merely an arm which is not yours, but several other arms. From that moment on, it's of no importance whether it's yours or not.

But, in any case, since, within a territory, people only know their own borders, they are not obliged to know that there are, say, six other territories along that border. They chuck them back however they like. There may thus be a ton of such territories.

It is certainly worth keeping in mind that a relationship may exist between the rejection of something and the birth of what I earlier called the master signifier. But in order for it to take on its full weight, there must clearly have been a chance accumulation of signifiers at certain points. It is on that basis that we can conceive of something like the birth of a language.

What we see get constructed as the first way of propping up in writing what serves as language, gives us at least a certain idea of it. Everyone knows that the letter A is the inverted head of a bull, and that there are still traces of a certain number of elements like that one, which are mobile. It is important not to proceed too quickly and to see where the holes remain. For example, it is quite clear that the starting point of this sketch was already linked to something that 18 marks the body with a possible ectopia and circulation, which obviously remain problematic.

Here again, everything is always there. It is something quite palpable that we can still verify every day. Again this week, very pretty photographs, that everyone savored, appeared in the newspaper, showing the impressive number of ways one human being can cut up another. That is where it all started.

There is another hole. As you know, people have tried to wrap their heads around Hegel. They have pointed out that Hegel's work is very nice, but that there is nevertheless something he doesn't explain. He explains the dialectic of the master and the slave, but he doesn't explain how there can be a society (made up) of masters. What I just explained to you is interesting insofar as, owing to the simple play of projection or chucking back, it is clear that, after a certain number of moves there will certainly be, I would say, a higher number of signifiers in certain territories than in others.

In any case, it remains to be seen how the signifier is going to be able to create a society (made up) of signifiers in this territory. It is important to never leave on the sidelines what you don't explain, with the excuse that you have managed to give a first explanatory sketch of it. Whatever the case may be, my title this year, "On a discourse that might not be a semblance" [or: "On a discourse that would (like) not (to) be based on semblance" (*du semblant*)], concerns something that has to do with an economy.

Here *du semblant* does not mean semblance of something else, but should be understood as an objective genitive [i.e., On a discourse . . . about (or: on) semblance]. At stake here is semblance as the very object that regulates the economy of discourse.

Am I going to say that it is also a subjective genitive [i.e., semblance's discourse]? Does *du semblant* also concern what holds discourse together? The word "subjective" must be ruled out here for the simple reason that a subject only appears once links between signifiers have been instated somewhere. A subject can only be the product of signifying articulation. The subject as such never, in any case whatsoever, masters this articulation, but is, strictly speaking, determined by it.

A discourse, by its very nature, *fait semblant* [pretends, constitutes semblance, or makes believe] – just as one can say that *il fait florès*, it is successful, *il fait léger*, it is light, not substantial, or *il fait chic*, it looks chic. If speech that is enunciated is true – because it is always very authentically what it is, at the level we are at, that of the objective and of articulation – then semblance is established as the specific object of what is produced solely in the said discourse.

19 Hence, the utterly meaningless character of what is articulated. It is here that the richness of language is revealed. It contains a logic that goes far beyond what we manage to crystallize out of it or detach from it.

I employed the hypothetical form by enunciating, "D'un discours qui ne *serait* pas du semblant" [*serait* is a conditional tense of the verb *être*: "On a discourse that might not be (or *would* like not to *be*) about semblance"]. Everyone knows what was done in logic after Aristotle's time regarding hypotheticals: everything that was articulated giving the value "true" or "false" to the articulation of the hypothesis, and combining what results from the implication, within this hypothesis, regarding a term that is indicated to be true. It is the inauguration of what is known as the modus ponens and of plenty of other modes, and you know what was done with them.

It is striking that no one anywhere – at least, as far as I know – has ever done anything with the negative use of this hypothetical. This is striking if you refer, for example, to what I included in my *Écrits*.

When, long ago, someone – at that heroic time when I began to clear the analytic ground – contributed to the deciphering of *Verneinung* by commenting on Freud's paper letter by letter, he realized very clearly – for Freud says it explicitly – that *Bejahung* only involves a judgment of attribution [not a judgment of existence]. In saying so, Freud shows a subtlety and a competence that were quite exceptional at the time he was writing, for only a few, not-very-well-known logicians could have highlighted it back then. A judgment of attribution doesn't imply existence, whereas a simple *Verneinung* implies the existence of the very thing that is negated. *D'un discours qui ne serait pas du semblant* posits that discourse, as I just stated, *is* about semblance.

The great advantage of putting it like that is that we don't say semblance "of what." This is what I propose to make headway regarding, namely – "what is at stake where *it might not be* [or: *it would like not to be*] about semblance"?

Naturally, the ground here has been prepared by an astonishing, albeit timid, step that Freud took in *Beyond the Pleasure Principle*.

All I can do here is indicate the knot formed in this statement by repetition and jouissance. It is owing to this that repetition violates the pleasure principle – which, I would say, never manages to get back up on its feet again. In light of psychoanalytic experience, hedonism can just go back to being what it is – namely, a philosophical myth. By which I mean a myth of a perfectly well-defined and clear class of myths, about which I stated last year that the help they provided to certain of the master's proceedings allowed the master's discourse as such to construct a form of knowledge. That knowledge, which is a master's knowledge, presupposed – and philosophical discourse still bears the marks of this – the existence, across from the master, of another knowledge. Thank God, philosophical discourse did not disappear before having first indicated that there must, at the outset, have been a relationship between that knowledge and jouissance. He who thus put an end to philosophical discourse – namely, Hegel – only sees the way in which the slave, through his work, manages to bring the master's knowledge into being.

So what does Freud's hypothesis, as I will call it, introduce that is new? In an extremely prudent form, which is nevertheless syllogistic, it is the following: If we call the pleasure principle the fact that, through their behavior, living beings always return to a minimal level of excitation, and we say that this principle regulates their economy; and if it turns out that repetition occurs in such a way that a dangerous jouissance is constantly brought into the picture, which goes beyond this minimal excitation; is it possible – Freud raises the question in this form – for us to think that life, considered in its cycle (this is a novelty with regard to our world that does not involve it universally), involves the possibility of repetition, repetition that would be the return to this world inasmuch as it is semblance?

You will immediately observe, thanks to what I am drawing on the blackboard, that this involves – instead of a series of rising and falling curves of excitation [Figure 1.1], all bordering on an upper limit – the possibility of an intensity of excitation that can also go to infinity [Figure 1.2].

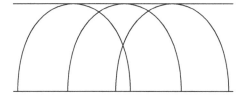 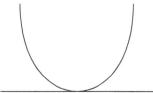

Figure 1.1 Rising and   Figure 1.2 Lower Tangency
       Falling Curves   Point or "Supreme" Point

Indeed, what is conceptualized as jouissance does not in and of itself involve any other limit, in theory, than this lower tangency point that we will call *suprême* [supremum or "least upper bound"], giving its proper meaning to this word that means the lowest point of an upper limit, just as *infime* [infimum or "greatest lower bound"] is the highest point of a lower limit.

This mortal point is thus conceived, without Freud highlighting it, as a characteristic of life. But, in truth, what no one actually realizes is that we thus confuse death with the status of nonlife, which does anything but sit still. The eternal silence of infinite spaces, which astonished Pascal, speak, sing, and stir now in all sorts of ways before our eyes. The so-called inanimate world is not death. Death is a point, an endpoint – of what? Of the jouissance of life.

This is precisely what was introduced by Freud's statement that we characterize as "hyperhedonism," if I may express myself thusly. Who can fail to see that economics – even the so-called economics of nature – is always a fact of discourse [or: created by discourse, *un fait de discours*]; and that discourse cannot grasp the fact that this indicates that jouissance is involved here solely insofar as it is itself not only a fact, but also an effect of discourse.

If something that is known as the unconscious can be half-spoken qua linguistic structure, it is in order that the outline [*relief*] of this effect of discourse, a discourse which hitherto seemed impossible to us, finally appears to us – namely, surplus jouissance. Does this mean, to employ one of my own formulations, that insofar as it seemed impossible, it functioned as real? I am raising the question, for in truth nothing implies that the irruption of the discourse of [or: about] the unconscious, as much as it continues to babble [or: remains incipient, *balbutiant*], implies anything about what preceded it, which was subjected to its structure. The discourse of the unconscious is an emergence, the emergence of a certain signifying function. It existed prior to that as a sign [*enseigne*], which is why I situated it for you at the core of semblance.

But the consequences of its emergence are what need to be introduced in order for something to change – which cannot change, for it is not possible. On the contrary, it is on condition that a discourse be centered around its effect as impossible that it would have some chance of being a discourse that would not be about semblance.

January 13, 1971

II

MAN AND WOMAN

The symptom, from Freud to Marx
The place of semblance in discourse
I am not a nominalist
Stoller and transsexualism
Saintliness, from Gracián to Mencius

I was looking for these papers, not in order to check something [m'assurer], but to reassure myself [me rassurer] about what I said last time, the typed-up text of which I don't have right now – something I just complained about.

Without me asking what they thought of it, a number of people made the following type of comment. At a few points in my last class, folks apparently wondered where I was going with this, as they put it.

I was also informed that people can't hear very well in the back of the room. I had no idea last week – I thought the acoustics here were just as good as in our last auditorium. If you would be so kind as to give me a sign when, in spite of myself, my voice drops, I will do my best to speak up.

At certain points last time, people thus wondered where I was going with this. In truth, such a question strikes me as premature enough to be significant – especially since those who said it are hardly inconsequential. A number of very well-informed people said it, and some of them even had no qualms about repeating it to me. Given what I discussed last time, it might be more germane to wonder where I am starting from, or even where I want to get you to start from. That already has two different meanings. It might mean to start from in order to go somewhere with me, and, then again, it might mean to dislodge you from your bubble.

This "where I am going with this" is, in any case, exemplary of what I say about the Other's desire. *Che vuoi? Keskiveu?* [This is

Lacan's transcription of an informal French way of pronouncing "*Qu'est-ce qu'il veut?*" What does he want?] We obviously feel far more comfortable when it is immediately clear. This is an occasion
24   to note the factor of inertia constituted by *Che vuoi?* – at least when we can provide an answer. This is why we strive to keep it an open question in analysis.

I clearly pointed out last time, nevertheless, that I am not here in the position of an analyst, meaning, in short, that I feel obliged to answer the question. That said, I must indicate the reason for which I spoke.

1

I spoke about semblance, and I said something you don't hear every day.

I emphasized first that the semblance that presents itself as what it is, is the primary function of truth. There is a certain "I am speaking" that does that, and it is not superfluous to recall this to mind to properly situate truth, for truth poses many logical difficulties.

This is all the more important to recall to mind because, if there is something revolutionary in Freud's work – let it be said in order to designate, in this way, a certain tone, and I have already warned you about the abusive use of the word – if there was a moment at which Freud was revolutionary, it was when he brought to the fore a function that Marx, too, brought to the fore. The only thing they have in common is that they both considered a certain number of facts to be symptoms.

The dimension of the symptom is that it speaks. It speaks even to those who don't know how to hear it. It doesn't say everything even to those who do.

The turning point was the emphasis placed on the symptom. We experience it in a certain register, the one that has continued humming along, let us say, for centuries around the topic of knowledge [*connaissance*]. It can't be said that we are completely empty-handed now when it comes to knowledge. But we keenly sense what is outdated in the theory of knowledge when it comes to explaining how scientists arrive at their formulations. Physics, for example, currently provides models.

Now, running parallel to the evolution of science, we, for our part, are in a position that one might qualify as being on the road to some truth. This shows a certain heterogeneity of status between the registers of knowledge and truth – except that, in my teaching,
25   and there alone, their coherence (which is not self-evident, or that

is only self-evident to those who, in the practice of analysis, pile on even more semblance) is demonstrated. This is what I will try to articulate today.

I said something else as well last week. Semblance is not simply locatable and essential in order to designate the primary function of truth; it is impossible to qualify the status of discourse without referring to it.

I tried to give the term "discourse" weight last year by defining four discourses. Last time, I could only quickly remind you of the name of one of them, the master's discourse, and certain people found that they were losing their footing at that point. What is to be done? I am not going to restate, even very quickly, what is at issue, even though I will return to it. As regards the function of discourse such as I formulated it last year, I already mentioned that you can read the answers I gave in a text entitled "Radiophonie" in the latest issue of *Scilicet*.

A discourse is constituted by four special places, one of which remained unnamed – the one that, owing to the function of its occupant, provides the name of each of the discourses. It is when the master signifier, S_1, is in a certain place that I am talking about the master's discourse. When a certain form of knowledge, S_2, occupies it, I am talking about university discourse. When the subject in its division, $\$$, which founds the unconscious, is in that place, I am talking about the hysteric's discourse. Lastly, when surplus jouissance, a, occupies it, I am talking about the analyst's discourse.

I will now give this, in some sense, sensitive [or: important, *sensible*] place – the one in the upper left-hand corner for those who were here and still remember, the one that is occupied by the signifier qua master, S_1, in the master's discourse, the place that I have not yet designated – a name, the name it deserves. That name is semblance.

This is to say, after what I stated last time, to what extent the signifier is, in that discourse, in its rightful place, as it were. Hence the success of the master's discourse. Yet this success is worth looking into for a moment, for who can believe that any master ever ruled by force? Especially at the outset, because, as Hegel reminds us, in his admirable hand-waving, one man is as good as another. If the master's discourse constitutes the ground, structure, and high point around which several civilizations were organized, it is because its mainspring is, all the same, something other than violence.

This is not to say that we are at all sure how things worked in primitive societies. We must exercise extreme caution when articulating facts. As soon as we label them with any term – "primitive," "prelogical," "archaic," or anything else, of whatever order – that is supposed to be *arche*, we have to wonder why *that* would be the beginning. Why wouldn't these primitive societies also be carryovers [*déchet*]? Nothing can help us answer that question.

They clearly show us, nevertheless, that things don't have to be based on the master's discourse. The mytho–ritual configuration, which is the best way to label them, does not necessarily imply the master's discourse. Yet it must be said that to be so interested in what is *not* the master's discourse is a certain kind of alibi. In most cases, it is a way of avoiding the issue – while we concern ourselves with that, we don't concern ourselves with something else. Nevertheless, the master's discourse is an essential logical ordering [*articulation*].

Some people, I'm not saying all of you, should try to wrap their heads around the way I expressed this ordering, for, as I clearly emphasized last time, whatever may happen that is new, and that is called revolutionary – I have always stressed that we must temper this term – can never involve anything more than a change in discourses [i.e., a rotation of terms, *déplacement du discours*].

To provide you with an image of this – despite the dumbing down images can bring with them – I would like to depict these places with four buckets, each of which has a name. A certain number of terms can slip into these buckets, namely, those that I pointed out: S_1, the master signifier; S_2, which, at the stage we are at, constitutes a certain body of knowledge; little *a*, insofar as it a direct consequence of the master's discourse; and $, which occupies, in the master's discourse, the place we are going to talk about today, and which I already named – the place of truth.

Truth is not the opposite [or: contrary, *contraire*] of semblance. Truth is the dimension, or *demansion* [a neologism, combining dimension and *mansio*, Latin for dwelling or abode; it might be rendered "dwelling place," "dwelling realm," or "dwealm"] – if you will allow me to coin a new word to designate these buckets – that is strictly correlated with the dimension of semblance. The *demansion* of truth props up that of semblance. Something is nevertheless specified regarding where this semblance is going with all this.

27   A question that is perhaps a bit beside the point came to my ears quite indirectly. Last time, it seems, two youngins – whom I salute if they are still here today, I hope they won't be offended that they were overheard – wondered, as they gravely shook their heads, "Is he a pernicious idealist?"

Am I a pernicious idealist? That strikes me as quite beside the point. I began by emphasizing – and it was quite an emphasis, for I said the exact opposite of what I meant to say – that discourse is an artifact. What I am sketching out with this is the exact opposite, for semblance is the opposite of artifact. As I pointed out, in nature, we find semblance everywhere. As soon as we are no longer talking about knowledge [*connaissance*] – as soon as people no longer believe that we know something through the pathway of perception, from which we extract some sort of quintessence, and realize, instead, that we know things by means of an apparatus known as discourse – the Idea is ruled out.

The first time the Idea appeared, it was actually a bit better situated than after Bishop Berkeley tried his hand at it. It was Plato who wondered wherein lay the reality of what we call a horse. His idea of the Idea involved the importance of the name [*dénomination*]. In this multiple and transitory thing, which was, moreover, far more obscure at his time than at ours, isn't the whole reality of a horse in the Idea, insofar as that means the signifier "a horse"?

We mustn't believe that Aristotle was much further along because he emphasized the reality of the individual. The individual means exactly what cannot be said. And up to a certain point, if Aristotle hadn't been the marvelous logician that he was – who took the unique and decisive step thanks to which we have a road map of what an articulated series of signifiers is – we might say, that, in his way of pointing out the nature of *ousia*, in other words, the real, he behaved like a mystic. The main characteristic of *ousia* is, as he himself says, that we can provide it with no attributes. It is not speakable. The unspeakable is the same as the mystical. He doesn't align himself with that viewpoint, but he leaves room for mysticism. It is obvious that Plato could not have solved the problem posed by the Ideas. It is in connection with functions and variables that a solution has been found.

If there is something that I am, it is clear that I am *not* a nominalist. By which I mean that my point of departure is not one implying that a name is something that is laminated onto reality. You have to make a choice. If you are a nominalist, you must completely give up on dialectical materialism, such that, in short, the nominalist tradition – which is, strictly speaking, the only danger of idealism that can be found in a discourse like mine – is quite obviously ruled out. The point is not to be a realist, like people were in the Middle Ages, in the sense of the realism of universals, but to indicate that our discourse, our scientific discourse, encounters reality [*réel*] only insofar as it relies on the function of semblance.

The algebraic articulation of semblance – which involves letters alone – and its effects constitute the only apparatus by which we designate what is real. What is real is what creates a hole in this semblance, in the articulated semblance constituted by scientific discourse. Scientific discourse makes headway without worrying any longer about whether it is semblance or not. All that matters is that its network, net, or "lattice," as they say, brings out the right holes in the right places. Its only point of reference is the impossible to which its deductions lead. The impossible is the real. The apparatus of discourse – insofar as it is discourse, in its rigor, that encounters the limits of its consistency – is that with which we aim, in physics, at something that is real.

What *we* are concerned with is the field of truth. Why is the field of truth, which can only be qualified in this way, of concern to us? I will try to articulate this today.

2

We, for our part, deal with something that differs from the real in physics. The thing for us that resists, is not open to any and every meaning, and is a consequence of our discourse is called "fantasy."

What we must test are its limits, structure, and function. The relationship in a discourse between little *a*, qua surplus jouissance, and $, the barred S of the subject – in other words, the exact relation that is blocked in the master's discourse – is what we have to test the functioning of when, in our thoroughly opposite position, that of the analyst's discourse, little *a* occupies the place of semblance and it is the subject who is situated across from little *a*. The place where the subject is questioned is the one where fantasy must take on its status, which is defined by the degree of impossibility there is in analytic questioning.

To clarify the status of "where I am going with this," I will turn to what I want to point out today regarding analytic theory. To do so, rather than to return to it, I am going to leave aside a function that was expressed in a certain manner of speaking that I adopted in addressing you here. Nevertheless, I can but draw your attention to the fact that, since, last time, I called you a name which seemed impertinent to many of you, and rightly so – crowded [or: freshly squeezed (or rushed)] surplus jouissance – should I now speak of some kind of freshly squeezed [word missing]? That nevertheless has a meaning, one my discourse – which is nothing like what Freud designated as the leader's discourse – preserves.

It is clearly at the level of discourse that Freud articulates – in his *Group Psychology and the Analysis of the Ego*, at the beginning of the 1920s – something that, oddly enough, turned out to be at the crux of the Nazi phenomenon. Recall the figure he provides at the end of Chapter 7, "Identification." The relations between capital I and little *a* are quite clearly indicated there. The figure truly seems to be designed to have Lacanian signs added to it.

That which, in a discourse, is addressed to the Other qua "You" [or: "Thou," *Tu*] brings on identification with something that we can call the human idol. If I spoke last time about real blood as the most useless blood with which to counteract semblance, it is clearly because one cannot take action to overthrow an idol without assuming its place immediately thereafter – this happened, as we know, to certain types of martyrs. In every discourse that appeals to "You," something provokes a hidden, secret identification, which is merely an identification with the enigmatic object; the latter can be nothing at all, Hitler's tiny surplus jouissance, which perhaps went no further than his mustache. This is what sufficed to crystallize people who were in no way mystics, who were quite thoroughly caught up in the workings of the capitalist's discourse, with everything it brings with it by way of a calling into question of surplus jouissance in its form as surplus value. People wanted to know whether, at a certain level, they would still have their little bit of it, and this was what sufficed to trigger the identification.

It is amusing that this took the form of an idealization of the 30 Aryan race – namely, of something that wasn't the least bit relevant. We can locate from whence this fictional character proceeds. But what we must simply say is that, for racism to be established, there is no need for this ideology – it is enough for there to be a surplus jouissance that is recognized as such.

Whoever looks even a little bit into what may happen in the future would do well to tell himself that every form of racism – insofar as a surplus jouissance suffices very well to prop it up – is now on the agenda. This is what we have coming to us in the years ahead. You will better understand why when I tell you what theory, the authentic use of analytic theory, allows us to formulate regarding surplus jouissance.

People imagine that they are saying something when they say that what Freud contributed is the idea that sexuality underlies everything related to discourse. People say that when they have been a little bit influenced by what I say about the importance of discourse in defining the unconscious, and they don't pay attention to the fact that I have not yet broached the status of the terms "sexuality" or "sexual relationship."

3

It is, of course, strange (*not* from but one single point of view, that of the charlatanism that presides over all therapeutic action in our society) that people have not noticed the huge gap that exists between the term "sexuality" – wherever it begins, where it merely begins, to take on a biological substance (and let me point out that, if there is a realm in which one can begin to perceive its meaning, it is the realm of bacteria) – and what Freud enunciates about the relations revealed by the unconscious.

Regardless of Freud's own stumblings regarding this topic, what he revealed about the functioning of the unconscious has nothing biological about it. It is only owing to what is known as a "sexual relationship" [or: "the relationship between the sexes," *rapport sexuel*] that something can be called "sexuality." This was, moreover, completely legitimate, until people began using the term "sexuality" to designate something else – namely, what is studied in biology, the chromosomes and their XY, XX, or XXY combinations. They have absolutely nothing to do with what is at issue, which has a perfectly pronounceable name: the relations between man and woman. We should take those two terms – in their fullest meanings, along with what they involve by way of a relation – as our point of departure.

We see the timid little attempts people make to think within the framework of a certain apparatus, which is that of psychoanalytic institutions. And when they perceive that not every question is settled by the debates that are considered divisive [*conflictuels*], they would really like something else, something "nonconflictual" – that's more relaxing. Then they notice, for example, that there is no need to wait for the phallic phase to begin in order to distinguish a little girl from a little boy; they are not at all the same long before that. They are astonished by this.

Since our next class won't be until the second Wednesday of February, you will perhaps have time to read something. If I recommend you read a book for once, it will perhaps have a bigger print run. It is entitled *Sex and Gender* by Robert J. Stoller. It is an interesting read, first of all, because, regarding an important subject, that of transsexuals, it provides a number of very well described case histories, along with their family coordinates. You are perhaps aware that transsexualism consists in the very energetic desire to change sexes by every possible means, even if that means undergoing operations when one is male. You will certainly learn many things about transsexualism from the book; the case studies that are included in it are altogether serviceable.

You will also see the completely unserviceable nature of the dialectical apparatus with which the author handles the topic, such that he has great difficulty explaining these cases, difficulties that arise right in front of his nose. One of the most surprising things is that the psychotic aspect of these cases is completely missed by the author, since he has no compass, never having heard of Lacanian foreclosure – something that could very easily explain the form taken by his cases. But no matter!

What is important is that "gender identity" is nothing other than what I just expressed with the terms "man" and "woman." It is clear that the question about what facet of gender identity appears before the phallic phase arises only because speaking beings are fated to be divided between men and women once they arrive at adulthood. In order to understand the emphasis that is placed on these things, on this instance, we have to realize that what defines man is his rela- 32 tionship to woman and vice versa. Nothing allows us to abstract the definitions of man and woman from our complete experience of speech, up to and including the institutions in which they are expressed – namely, marriage.

For a boy who reaches adulthood, the point is to play the part of a man [*faire-homme*]. That is what constitutes the relation to the other party. It is in light of this, something that constitutes a fundamental relation, that everything we wish to investigate in the child's behavior can be interpreted as oriented toward this playing the part of a man. One of its essential correlates is to signal to the girl that one is a man. In short, we immediately find ourselves in the dimension of semblance.

This is evinced by everything, including the references we find everywhere to sexual display – among the upper mammals, primarily, but also among four-legged vertebrates. A very large number of studies, delving deep into the animal phylum, show the essential character, in sexual relationships, of something that we should limit entirely to the level at which we encounter it – which is in no wise a cellular level, whether chromosomic or not, nor an organic level, whether we are talking about the ambiguity of one tract or another in the gonads – namely, the ethological level. This level is clearly that of semblance. The male is most often the agent of the display behavior, but the female is not absent since she is precisely the one who is affected by the display. It is because there is display that something takes place that is known as "copulation," which is no doubt sexual in its function, but whose status is that of a specific element of identity.

It is clear that human sexual behavior easily finds its reference point [or: compass reading, *référence*] in display, such as it is defined in the animal kingdom. It is clear that human sexual behavior conserves certain aspects of this animal semblance. The only thing that differentiates them is that, in humans, semblance is transmitted in a discourse; thus it is at the level of discourse, and at the level of discourse alone, that human sexual behavior is conveyed toward, if you will allow me, a certain effect that might not be a [or: might not be based on (or: not be mere)] semblance. This means that, instead of having the exquisite courtesy that animals have, men sometimes rape women and vice versa.

At the limits of discourse, insofar as discourse strives to hold that semblance together, something real occurs from time to time. This is what is known as a desperate act [*passage à l'acte*], and I can see no better place to designate what it means. Note that, in most cases, such desperate acts are carefully avoided. They only happen by accident.

It is also an opportunity to clarify what I have long differentiated from such desperate acts: "acting out." The latter consists in putting semblance on stage, raising it up to the level of the stage, and making an example of it. That is what is known as "acting out" in this realm. It is also known as passion.

I am obliged to move ahead quickly here, but you will note that, as I just clarified things, one can clearly point out something that I have always said – namely, that if discourse is there insofar as it allows for surplus jouissance as a stake [*enjeu*], it's very precisely (and here I'm going all the way) as what is prohibited in sexual discourse. There's no such thing as a sexual act. I have already said so several times, and I will broach it here from a different angle.

This is rendered quite palpable by the massive economy of analytic theory – namely, what Freud encounters, at first so innocently, as it were, that it is tantamount to a symptom. Namely, that he makes headway at the level of truth to the point at which things concern us. Who doesn't realize that the Oedipal myth is necessary for designating the real, for this is clearly what it aims to do? Or more precisely, what the theoretician is forced to admit, when he formulates this hypermyth, is that the real, strictly speaking, is incarnated on the basis of what? Sexual jouissance. As what? As impossible, since what Oedipus designates is a mythical being. A mythical being who enjoys what? All women.

Isn't the fact that such an artifice [*appareil*] is imposed on us here, in some sense, by discourse itself, the surest confirmation of my theoretical statement regarding the prevalence of discourse and the status of jouissance? What psychoanalytic theory articulates is something whose graspable nature as an object is what I designate as object little *a* insofar as, owing to a certain number of favorable organic contingencies, it comes to occupy the place [*remplir*] defined as that of surplus jouissance – breast, excrement, gaze, or voice.

What does the theory state, if not that the relationship to surplus jouissance is essential to the subject? It is in the name of this relationship that the mother becomes so prevalent in all analytic case

studies. In truth, surplus jouissance is only normalized on the basis
of a relationship that is established with sexual jouissance – with 34
the proviso that this jouissance is only formulated and articulated
on the basis of the phallus, insofar as the phallus is its signifier.
Someone wrote one day that the phallus is the signifier that designates the lack of a signifier. That's absurd – I never said any such
thing. The phallus is quite clearly sexual jouissance insofar as it
is coordinated with semblance, insofar as it is part and parcel of
semblance.

This is clearly the way it is, and it is quite strange to see all the
analysts endeavor to look the other way. Rather than having ever
more strongly emphasized the turning point or crisis of the phallic
phase, they do everything possible to ignore it. The truth that not
one of these young speaking beings can avoid facing is that there are
certain people who don't have a phallus [i.e., a penis]. This forces
them to deal with two lacks: the fact that there are people who don't
have one, and the fact that they were not aware of this truth up until
then. Sexual identification does not consist in believing oneself to be
a man or a woman, but in the boy taking into account the fact that
there are women, and the girl taking into account the fact that there
are men. What is important is not so much what they feel – it is a
real situation, if you will allow me. The fact is that for men, a girl
is the phallus, and that is what castrates them. For women, a boy
is the same thing, the phallus; and that is what castrates them, too,
because they only acquire a penis and that doesn't do the trick [c'est
râté]. Neither the boy nor the girl runs a risk at the outset, except
via the dramas they trigger – they are the phallus for a little while.

That is the reality [réel] of sexual jouissance, insofar as that jouissance is detached as such – it is the phallus. In other words, the
Name-of-the-Father. I scandalized certain pious people when I first
equated those two terms.

But there is something that is worth emphasizing a bit more.
What is the place of semblance, in the way semblance operates,
such as I just defined it at the level of the relationship between man
and woman? What is the place of archaic semblance? What is its
role which is, in fact, foundational? This is assuredly what makes it
worth dwelling a bit longer on what woman represents.

For man, in this relation, woman is precisely the moment of
truth. With regard to sexual jouissance, woman is in the position of
highlighting [or: punctuating, ponctuer] the equivalence between jouissance and semblance. Therein lies the distance between man and
her. If I spoke of the moment of truth, it is because it is the moment
to which man's whole education is designed to (cor)respond, by 35
maintaining his semblance at all costs. It is far easier for a man to

meet any rival on the battlefield than to confront a woman insofar as she is the medium [or: prop, *support*] of this truth, the medium of what there is by way of semblance in the relationship between man and woman.

In truth, the fact that semblance is jouissance to a man here indicates clearly enough that jouissance is semblance. It is because he is at the intersection of these two jouissances that a man maximally experiences discontent with the relationship designated as sexual – with, as the man said, "these pleasures known as physical."

On the other hand, no one knows better than a woman – and it is in this respect that she is the Other – what distinguishes jouissance from semblance. For she [or: jouissance, *elle*] is the presence of what she knows: namely, that while jouissance and semblance are equivalent in a certain dimension of discourse, they are nevertheless distinct in the test [or: trial, *épreuve*] that a woman represents for a man, the test of truth quite simply, the only one that can give semblance itself its rightful place.

It must be said that everything we have been told about the mainspring of the unconscious represents nothing but horror at this truth. That is what I am trying to explain to you today, as one does with Japanese flowers. It is not especially pleasant to hear, and it is what is usually packaged under the heading of the "castration complex." Because of the little label that is stuck on it, we can remain calm, set it aside, and never have anything further to say about it, if not that it is there and we tip our hat to it from time to time.

But the fact that a woman may be a man's truth – recall the proverb trotted out when we try to understand something, "*cherchez la femme*," to which people naturally give a detective interpretation – could well mean something quite different: in order to know a man's truth, one would do well to know who his woman is. I mean his wife in this case, and why not? It's the only case in which something somebody in my entourage once called the "bathroom scale" [*pèse-personne*] makes any sense. To size up [or: weigh, *peser*] a man, nothing beats sizing up his wife.

But when we talk about women, it's not the same, because women have a great deal of freedom with regard to semblance. They can manage to give weight even to a man who doesn't have any.

4

These are truths that have been known for centuries, but that are never repeated, except in private.

There is, of course, a whole literature on the topic, and we should know something about its scope. It is of no interest, naturally, unless one selects the best texts therein.

Baltasar Gracián, for example, was an eminent Jesuit who wrote things that are among the most intelligent one can write; somebody should prepare a study of his works someday.

Their intelligence is absolutely prodigious, insofar as what is at stake for him is to establish what one might call the holiness of man. His book, *The Courtiers Manual Oracle*, can be summarized very briefly: to be a saint. It is the only place in Western civilization where the word "saint" has the same meaning as in Chinese: *sheng-ren*, 圣人.

Take note of this because it is getting late and I will not be able to go into it today. I will provide a few references to the origin of Chinese thought this year.

I realized something, which is that I am perhaps Lacanian only because I studied Chinese back in the day. I mean that when I reread things that I had studied and repeated like an idiot wearing a dunce cap, I now realize that they are of a piece with what I talk about.

I will give an example from Mencius, who wrote one of the fundamental, canonical books of Chinese thought. One of his disciples begins saying things like "Don't go looking for what you don't find in *yan*, 言" – that is discourse – "in your spirit." I am translating by "spirit" the character *xin*, 心, which means the heart, but what it designated was clearly spirit, Hegel's *Geist* [mind or spirit]. Well, that would require a bit more explanation.

"And if you don't find what you are looking for in your spirit, don't go looking for it in your *zhi*" – in other words, your feelings [or: sensitivity (or sensations), *sensibilité*]. The Jesuits translated it as they could, getting a bit out of breath at that point.

I am only indicating these different levels in order to bring out the distinction, which is very strict, between what is articulated – discourse – and what is spirit – namely, the essential. If you have not already found what you are looking for at the level of speech, then it's hopeless – don't bother looking for it elsewhere, at the level of feelings [*sentiments*]. Mengzi, Mencius, contradicts himself – that is clear. But what we need to know is why and by what pathway.

I am saying this in order to indicate that a certain way of bringing discourse to the fore does not take us back to archaic things. In Mencius's time, discourse was already perfectly well articulated and constituted. It cannot be understood by taking it as some sort of primitive thought.

In truth, I have no idea what primitive thought is. Something that is far more concrete that we have within arm's reach is what is known as underdevelopment. But underdevelopment is not archaic; as everyone knows, it is produced by the expansion of capitalism. I would go even further: what we notice and what we will notice more and more is that underdevelopment is the very precondition for capitalist expansion. Seen from a certain angle, the October revolution itself provides proof thereof.

But what we must see is that we are dealing with a form of underdevelopment that is going to be ever more flagrant, ever more widespread. We must test whether the key to various problems that are going to present themselves isn't to situate ourselves at the level of the effect of capitalist articulation that I left in the shadows last year, giving you but the root of it in the master's discourse. I may be able to provide a little bit more this year.

We have to see what we can extract from what I will call an "underdeveloped logic." This is what I am trying to articulate here before you "for your better usage," as the Chinese texts put it.

January 20, 1971

III

AGAINST THE LINGUISTS

The referent is never the right one
Linguistics is untenable
Double articulation in Chinese
Metonymy as a prop for surplus jouissance
Between *hsing* and *ming*

Owing to the strike, people asked me if I was going to hold my seminar. There were even two, or perhaps only one, but maybe two people who asked my opinion about the strike, or rather who contacted my secretary. Well I ask you: Does anyone have anything to say in favor of the strike, at least with regard to this Seminar? I am not going to leave those of you who are present today in the lurch.

I was rather tempted to go on strike this morning, however. I was inclined to because my secretary showed me a little article in the newspaper concerning the call for a strike, to which was added, given the paper in question, a communiqué from the Ministry of National Education detailing everything that has been done for the French university system, the average number of teachers that have been employed per number of students, etc. I won't go so far as to contest the statistics. However, the conclusion that was drawn from them – which was that this huge effort should, in any case, satisfy the students – does not concur with my sources, which are nevertheless quite reliable.

I was rather inclined to go on strike because of that. Your presence here will force me to give my Seminar, owing to something important. It is what we, in our tongue, call "courtesy," and what, in another tongue – one that I announced I would refer to, in order to entice you, in a sense, to come back – namely, Chinese, is called *yi*, 義. I let myself go so far as to confide in you that I had studied a bit of Chinese back in the day.

Yi, in the grand tradition, is one of the four cardinal virtues. Whose virtues? Virtues of what? Of a man at a certain time. And if I am speaking about them in this way, as it strikes me, it's because I felt I had some rather informal things to say to you; that is, moreover, how I think I will speak to you today. It isn't strictly what I had prepared. I will thus take the strike into account in my own way. You will see at what level I will situate things. I will do so more informally, in order to answer equitably. This is about the best meaning one can give to *yi* – to respond in an equitable manner to your presence.

I will, as you will see, take advantage of this to broach a number of points that have been equivocal for some time. Since something is, moreover, at issue regarding the university system, I believe I should also comment on that, whereas, in many cases, I don't deign [*je dédaigne*] to mention social movements I hear about.

1

As you perhaps know – does your presence here attest to this or not? how would I know? – I am, in relation to the said university system, in a position that is merely marginal, let us say. Since that system feels that it must provide me a podium, I certainly must pay it homage. And yet something has been manifesting itself for some time that I can't ignore, given the field in which I happen to teach. I hear echoes, noises, and murmurs from an academically defined field known as linguistics.

When I speak of disdain [*dédain*], I'm not talking about a feeling, but rather a behavior. About two years ago, which is not very far back, an article came out in a journal that no one reads anymore – the journal's name, the *Nouvelle Revue Française*, thus sounds outdated – an article entitled "Jacques Lacan's stylistic exercises." It was an article that I even pointed out to you in my Seminar two years ago. At that time I was teaching at the *École Normale* – under its roof, or, rather, its awning, standing at the threshold – and I told you to read it because it's funny. It turned out, as you saw later, not to be as funny as it seemed, because I should have realized that it was a bell tolling to signal to me, even though I am deaf, confirmation of something that I'd already been told – that there was no longer any room for me under that awning. I could have taken note of that confirmation, because it was written in that article.

The guy wrote something quite hard to believe, I must say, namely, that people could hope that, when I would no longer be under the *École Normale*'s awning, linguistics – high-quality, advanced linguistics, that sort of thing – would be taught at that *École*. I'm not sure I am citing his exact terms; you can be sure I didn't reread it this morning, since all of this is extemporaneous. Something perhaps told him that linguistics was, by Jove, compromised at the heart of the *École Normale*. In the name of what, good Lord! I had no assigned teaching role at the *École Normale*, so if, as this author claimed, people there happened to be so unfamiliar with linguistics, it was certainly not my doing.

This brings me to what I intend to highlight this morning. A question has, in fact, been arising for some time now, even somewhat insistently, and the topic has been taken up again in a less frivolous way in a certain number of interviews: "Is someone a structuralist or not when he is a linguist?" When people want to differentiate themselves, they say they are functionalists. Why do they say that? Because structuralism – which is a purely journalistic invention, as I told you [Seminar XVI, p. 3] – serves as a label. And given what it includes, namely, a certain seriousness, it can't help but worry people. Which leads them, naturally, to want to point out that they reserve seriousness for themselves.

I want to foreground the relationship between linguistics and what I teach, so as to dissipate a certain equivocation, in a way that will, I hope, be taken notice of.

Academic linguists would, in short, like to reserve the right to speak about language for themselves. The fact that my teaching revolves around recent work in linguistics means that there is thus something brazen about it, and this objection is formulated in various ways. The main formulation – the one that is, at least it seems to me, the most consistent – states that people make (at least the author sets out to prove this), and I quote, "metaphorical use" of linguistics in the field that happens to be the one I work in, as well as in Lévi-Strauss's field, for example. The latter would certainly deserve to be examined a bit more closely when the opportunity arises, far more closely than what I teach, for people may have but rather vague notions about it. 42

Thus, Lévi-Strauss, and a few others too – including Roland Barthes and myself – are said to make metaphorical use of linguistics. It is here that I would like to make [or: score, *marquer*] a few points.

We should begin – because it is nevertheless inscribed in something that counts – from the fact that I am still here proffering this discourse, and that you are also here to hear it. A certain formulation regarding the discourse I proffer can't be completely out of place: let us say that I know – but what? Let us try to be accurate – it seems proven that "I know what's what" [or: "I know what to expect," *Je sais à quoi m'en tenir*]. Let me highlight that the specific place I occupy [*la tenue d'une certaine place*] is no other – I am highlighting this because I am not stating it for the first time, I spend my time repeating that this is what I hold fast to [*de là que je me tiens*] – than the place I designate as that of an analyst. The point can, after all, be debated – many psychoanalysts would contest it – but that is where I stand.

To state "I know where I stand" [*Je sais où je me tiens*] is not quite the same as to state *Je sais à quoi m'en tenir* – not because the "I" is repeated in the second part of the former sentence, and this is where the richness of language always shines through – but because when I say "I know where I stand," the accent of what I take pride in knowing goes on the word "where." It would be as if I had a map of the place. And why wouldn't I, after all?

There is a very good reason why I cannot even claim to know where I stand. This is truly in the vein of what I wish to talk with you about this year. It is because no one in any core field of science, as it is currently proceeding – I am talking about what I refer to when I situate Newtonian science at its center, the introduction of the Newtonian field – has a map that can tell us where we are. Moreover – and everyone agrees on this – as soon as we begin to talk about a map, about its randomness and its necessity, anyone can object, regardless of the validity of the yardstick employed, that we are no longer doing science but philosophy. This does not mean that everyone knows what they are saying when they say that. They nevertheless have a point.

Scientific discourse repudiates this "where we are at." That is not what it operates with. The hypotheses – recall that Newton claimed that he didn't frame any [*hypotheses non fingo*] – employed, however, 43 never concern the foundation of things. In the scientific realm, and regardless of what people think, hypotheses have to do with logic. There is an "if," the conditional [or: protasis] of a truth that is never anything but logically articulated. And then there is the apodosis – a consequent must be verifiable, verifiable at its level, such as it is articulated. This proves nothing about the truth of the hypothesis.

I am certainly not saying that science floats on the surface like a pure construction, and that it has no impact on reality [*ne mord pas sur le réel*]. To say that it does not prove the truth of an hypothesis is simply to recall to mind that implication in logic does not in any way imply that true conclusions can't be drawn from false premises. The fact remains that the truth of an hypothesis in an established scientific field can be recognized by the way it orders the whole field, insofar as it has its status. This status cannot be defined otherwise than on the basis of the consent of all those who have recognized credentials [*autorisés*] in that scientific field; the status involved here is, thus, academic.

This may appear far-fetched [or: overly sweeping, *grosses*]. But the fact remains that it is what explains that university discourse can be formulated as I strove to formulate it last year. Now, it is clear that the way I formulated it is the only one that allows us to perceive why it is no accident, not owing to some random event, that scientific advancement involves the presence and support of other social entities that we know well – the army, for example, or the Marines, as people still say, and several other like elements. It is altogether legitimate for us to see that university discourse can only be formulated on the basis of the master's discourse.

It is only in the distribution of departments in a field whose status is academic that we can ask what is happening and whether it is possible for a discourse to be labeled differently.

Pardon me for beginning anew from such an elementary point. But, after all, since objections – as huge as the one that I merely make a metaphorical use of linguistics – are made to me by people who are authorized to do so because they are linguists, I must respond, regardless of the occasion on which I do so.

I am doing so this morning because I was expecting to encounter a more combative atmosphere here.

2

I must, thus, recall to mind the following.

Can I, in all decency, say that I know? That I know what? Because, after all, perhaps I situate myself in a place that Mencius, whose name I mentioned last time, could help us define.

If "I know what's what" [or: "I know what to expect," *Je sais à quoi m'en tenir*], I still have to say simultaneously, and may Mencius protect me, that I don't know what I am saying. In other words, what I can't say is that "I know what I am saying." That has been true since Freud arrived on the scene and introduced the concept of the unconscious.

The unconscious doesn't mean anything if it doesn't mean that – regardless of what I say, and regardless of where I stand, even if I stand up straight [or: behave correctly, *tiens bien*] – I don't know what I am saying, and that none of the discourses, such as I defined them last year, leaves us any hope, or allows anyone to claim, or even hope in any way, to know what he is saying.

Even if I don't know what I am saying – at least I know that I don't know it, and I am not the first to say things under such conditions, we've heard it before [from Socrates] – I say that the reason for this must be sought out in language itself. What I add to Freud – even if it is already there in Freud's work, and patently so, because everything he demonstrates having to do with the unconscious involves linguistic material, and linguistic material alone – is that the unconscious is structured like a language. Which one? Well, look for it.

I will speak [*causerai*] to you in [or: about] French or Chinese. At least I would like to. It is only too clear that, at a certain level, what I cause is bitterness, specifically in linguists. This inclines us to think that having academic status turns linguistics into an odd sort of hodgepodge, as is only too obvious from its current course. Given what we see, there can be no doubt about it. The fact that people point the finger at me in this case is, good Lord, hardly important. The fact that people don't debate my work is not very surprising either, because I don't and cannot take my stand on the basis of an academically defined field.

What is amusing is that it is obvious that a certain number of people – among whom I situated myself earlier by adding two other names, Claude Lévi-Strauss and Roland Barthes, to the list, and I could add still others – have sparked considerable growth in the number of jobs in linguistics (a number that was listed this morning in the paper by the Ministry of National Education), as well as in the number of its students.

The wave of interest in linguistics that I have contributed to is, it seems, an interest on the part of ignoramuses. Well, that's not such a bad thing. They were ignorant before, and now they are interested. I have managed to interest the ignorant in something more, which was not my goal because I myself couldn't care less about linguistics. What specifically interests me is language, because it is what I believe I deal with when I conduct an analysis.

It is the job of linguists to define the object of linguistics. Each scientific field advances by defining its object. Linguists define theirs as they like, and they add that I make a metaphorical usage of it. It is truly odd that linguists don't realize that any and every usage of language, whatever it may be, occurs in the realm of metaphor, there being no language that is not metaphorical. Any attempt to "metalanguage" something, if I may put it thusly, demonstrates this. All it can do is try to begin from what people always define, whenever they try to make headway in a so-called logical direction – namely, an object-language [see Bertrand Russell, among others]. Now, in the statements made in any one of these logical attempts, we clearly see that this object-language is ungraspable [or: can't be pinned down, *insaisissable*]. It is of the very nature of language – I am not saying of speech, I am saying of language itself – that when we try to broach anything that signifies in it, the referent is never the right one, and that is what constitutes a language.

Every designation is metaphorical; it can only occur via something else. Even if I say "It" [*Ça*] as I point to my cigar, I am already implying, by calling it "It," that I am choosing to make of it a mere "It," whereas it is not "It." The proof is that, when I light it, it is something else even at the level of "It" [or: id, *Ça*], the famous "It" that would be the individual's last holdout [or: refuge, *réduit*]. We cannot overlook the fact that to say "It" is a fact of language. What I just designated as "It" is not my cigar. It is "It" when I smoke it, but when I smoke it, I don't talk about it.

The signifier "It" to which discourse refers, in this case, when there is discourse – and it seems that we can hardly escape from discourse – this signifier may well be the only prop of some thing. By its very nature, it evokes a referent. Yet it cannot be the right 46 one. This is why the referent is always real, because it is impossible to designate. Thanks to which we can but construct it. And we construct it if we can.

There is no reason for me to remind you of what you all know, because you read it in the pile of occult junk that you lap up, as everyone knows – isn't it true? I am talking about *yin* and *yang*. Like everyone else, you've heard of those, haven't you? Male and female. They make for very pretty little characters. The one I am drawing here is *yang*. I will draw *yin* for you another time.

yang

I will draw it for you another time because I don't see why I should make excessive use of these Chinese characters that mean something to only a very few of you. I will make use of them nevertheless.

We are not here to engage in wangling. If I speak to you about *yin* and *yang*, it is because they are examples of unlocatable referents. This doesn't mean they that they aren't fucking real. The proof is that we are still weighed down by them.

If I make a metaphorical use of linguistics, it is because the unconscious cannot conform to a kind of research – I mean linguistics – that is untenable. That doesn't stop us from exploring it, of course – that's a wager we make. Yet I have already made enough use of wagers [e.g., Pascal's] for you to know, or rather for you to suspect, that this may serve some purpose. Losing is just as important as winning.

Linguistics can only be a metaphor that is constructed in order not to work. But in the end, it interests us a great deal, because – as you will see, I am announcing that this is what I will talk to you about this year – psychoanalysis sails full speed ahead in the same metaphor. That is precisely what encouraged me to return, just like that – after all, we know what it's worth – to the little Chinese I learned long ago. Why, after all, wouldn't I have understood it not too badly when I studied it with my dear Professor Demiéville? I was already a psychoanalyst at the time.

47

wei

This character is read *wei* and is also part of the formulation *wu wei*, which means nonaction [*non-agir*]. *Wei* thus means to act, but it can easily be used to mean "as" [or: like, *comme*], too. It means "as," in other words, it serves as a conjunction with which to create a metaphor, and it also means "insofar as it refers to something specific," which goes even further in the direction of metaphor. Indeed, to say that it refers to something is to say that it is not part and parcel of it, since it is required to refer to it. When one thing refers to another, the widest berth or flexibility is given to the possible use of this term "*wei*," which nevertheless means "to act."

A tongue like that isn't bad, a tongue in which the verbs and the "surplus verbs" [*plus-verbes*] – what can be more verb [*plus verbe*], more of an active verb than "to act" [*agir*]? – regularly transform into minute conjunctions. That helped me a great deal to generalize the function of the signifier, even if it pokes in the ribs a few linguists who don't know Chinese.

To a certain linguist who has talked about nothing but double articulation for the past few years – he's killing us with it – I would like to ask, for example, what he does with it in Chinese, huh?

For you see, in Chinese the first articulation is all alone and produces meaning all by itself. Since all of the words are monosyllabic, you can't say that the phoneme means nothing while words mean something, there being two articulations and two levels. For in Chinese, there is meaning even at the phonemic level.

This doesn't mean that, when you put several phonemes – each of which already means something – together, you don't get a bigger word with several syllables (just like in our tongue), a word that has a meaning, one that bears no relation to what each of the phonemes mean. Double articulation is a hoot here.

It's funny that people forget that there is a language like that when they claim that the function of double articulation is characteristic of all language. I'm willing to admit that everything I say is nonsense, but let them tell me why. May a linguist stand up here and tell me how double articulation holds true in Chinese. 48

So I am very gently introducing this *wei* to you, to get you used to it. I will provide a minimum of other terms, too, which will hopefully serve some purpose. The fact that this term is both the verb to act [*agir*] and the conjunction involved in metaphor lightens our load, moreover. Perhaps *im Anfang war die Tat*, as Goethe said, perhaps "in the beginning was the act [or: action (or deed)]"; that is perhaps exactly equivalent to saying *en arche*, "in the beginning was the Word." The word is, perhaps, the only "action" there is.

What is insane is that I can guide you like that for a long time with metaphor, and the further I go, the more you will be misled, because it is the nature of metaphor not to travel alone. There is also metonymy that functions simultaneously, and even while I am talking to you, because it's still metaphor that . . . – as very competent and nice people, who are known as linguists, say.

Linguists are so competent that they have even been forced to invent the notion of "competence." Language [*langue*] is competence incarnate. Moreover, it is true: we are competent in nothing else.

Yet, as they themselves have also noticed, the only way to prove it is through performance. They are the ones who call it "performance." I don't. I have no need to. I am performing right now, even as I speak to you about metaphor. And naturally, I dupe you because the only interesting thing is what occurs during a performance – namely, that surplus jouissance is produced: yours and the surplus jouissance that you attribute to me when you reflect.

3

You occasionally reflect. You do it above all when you wonder what the hell I'm doing here. I can't help but believe that it gives you pleasure, at the level of the surplus jouissance that makes you crowd in here [*qui vous presse*].

As I have already explained, this is the level at which the operation of metonymy occurs, thanks to which you can be led by the nose almost anywhere – not just out into the hallway, naturally.

But leading you out into the hallway, or even beating you in the town square, is not what is of interest. What is of interest is to keep you here in nice neat rows, crowded together, and squeezed against 49 each other. While you are here, you aren't doing anyone any harm. Such banter can take us rather far, because we can try to articulate the function of *yin* on its basis.

What's the story behind surplus jouissance? Let me remind you as I can.

It's obvious that surplus jouissance could only be defined, as it was by me, on the basis of what? A serious formulation of the object relation, such as it can be isolated in the experience known as Freudian. That does not suffice. It required that I make that relation flow, providing it with a bucket made out of Marx's surplus value, something no one had ever thought of doing. Marx's surplus value cannot be grasped all that easily. If it was invented, it is in the sense in which the word "invention" means that one finds something good neatly ensconced in a little corner – in other words, that it is a real find. For it to be a real find, it had to already be well polished and broken in by what? By a discourse. Thus, surplus jouissance, like surplus value, can only be detected in a developed discourse, it being out of the question to debate whether it can be defined as the capitalist's discourse.

You are not very curious, and above all, not very interventionist. When I talked to you about the master's discourse last year, no one came to ask me how the discourse of the capitalist fits into that. I was expecting it. I'd love to explain it to you, especially since it's as easy as pie. All you have to do is flip a little gismo and your master's discourse proves to be something that can easily be transformed into the capitalist's discourse.

But that is not what is important. Marx himself clearly showed that the capitalist's discourse is closely connected to the master's discourse. Where I am going with this is to get you to grasp something that is essential here: the prop of surplus jouissance.

You are all aware that I don't provide you with very many props. They are what I most mistrust, for it is with such things that we make the worst extrapolations. In short, it is with such things that people do psychology, which is truly necessary if we are to manage to conceptualize the function of language. Thus, when I make metonymy the prop of surplus jouissance, I am entirely justified. What makes you follow me is the fact that this surplus jouissance is essentially a slippery object. It is impossible to stop its sliding at any point in a sentence.

But why not allow ourselves to perceive that it is utilizable in a discourse – it's all the same to me whether it is linguistic or not, as I already said – which is mine, and that it is utilizable only insofar as it is borrowed, not from the capitalist's discourse, but from capitalist logic? This brings us back to something I said last time that left a few of you a bit perplexed. Everyone knows that I always end my classes with a little gallop, because I perhaps dawdle or drag my feet a bit too much beforehand. Certain people tell me that. What can I say? Everybody has his own rhythm. That is how I make love.

I talked to you about an underdeveloped logic. That left a few of you scratching your heads. What is an underdeveloped logic going to look like?

Let us begin with the following. Last time, I clearly indicated that the expansion of capitalism brings underdevelopment with it. I will put it differently today. I confided in someone that I met at the exit, saying to him, "I would've liked to illustrate it by saying that Mr. Nixon is, in fact, Mr. Houphouët-Boigny in person." "Oh," he said to me, "you should've said so." So I'm saying it now. The only difference between the two of them is that Nixon underwent analysis, or so I hear. You see what that leads to. When someone has been analyzed in a certain way – and this is always true in every single case, when he has been psychoanalyzed in a certain way, in a certain field, in a certain school, by people we can name – he becomes incurable. We must call a spade a spade, all the same. He becomes incurable.

This has considerable consequences. For example, someone who has been psychoanalyzed somewhere, in a certain place, by certain people, who can be named, not by just any old analyst – well, it's out of the question that he understand a word of what I say. I've seen this proven time and again. Books come out every day that prove it. This alone raises questions, nevertheless, regarding the possibilities of performance when it functions in a certain discourse.

If discourse is sufficiently developed, then you have a relationship with some thing – let us say, leaving it at that – and it just so happens that this thing interests you. But that is purely by accident and no one knows about your relation to it. Here's how it is written:

xing

51

The classic French transcription of this is "*sing*." If you place an "h" in front of it, you get the English transcription, which is also the most recent Chinese transcription, if I am not mistaken, because, after all, it's purely conventional – it is now written "*xing*." Of course, it is not pronounced "*xing*," it is pronounced "*sing*."

It is nature. It is the nature that I am far from excluding from the picture, as you may have seen. If you are not completely stone-deaf, you might have noticed that the first thing worth remembering in what I told you at our first meeting this year is that the signifier is rampant in nature. I talked to you about the stars, about constellations more precisely, because stars aren't all the same. For centuries, the sky was it: 天. It's the first line, the top horizontal one, that is important. It's a platter or a blackboard. People reproach me for using the blackboard. It's all that's left to us of the heavens, my friends, which is why I use it to write what must serve as your constellations.

It thus results from a sufficiently developed discourse that all of you – whether you're here or in the USA or elsewhere, it's all the same – are underdeveloped with regard to this discourse. I am talking about something we must take an interest in, and which is certainly what we are talking about when we talk about your underdevelopment. Where exactly should it be situated? What should we say about it? We are not doing philosophy by wondering what the substance of what is happening is. We find commentary on that in the work of our old friend Mencius.

I don't see, after all, any reason to pump you full of this [or: fill your heads with this (or get you doped up on this), *vous faire droguer*], since I truly have no hope that you will take the trouble to read his work. I will thus go into something – why not? – that I should organize into three ranked stages, especially since Mencius tells us things that are extraordinarily interesting. Moreover, we don't know how things come out, because it is constructed God only knows how. This book by Mencius is a collage, things come out one after another, but don't resemble each other, as they say [cf. the French expression *les jours se suivent mais ne se ressemblent pas*; "days follow one another, but don't resemble each other"]. In short, 52 alongside the notion of *xing*, nature, the notion of *ming*, heaven's decree, suddenly comes out:

ming

I could, of course, just stick with *ming*, heaven's decree – in other words, continue talking. Which would, in short, mean: that's the way it is because that's the way it is; one day science grew in our field. Contemporaneously, capitalism began to act up; and then there was a guy – God only knows why, it must have been heaven's decree – named Marx who, in short, assured capitalism a rather long life. And then there was Freud who suddenly began to investigate something that manifestly became the only interesting element that still had something to do with the knowledge [*connaissance*], as it was known, that people had dreamt about before. At a time when there was no longer a trace of anything with any such meaning, Freud perceived that there were symptoms.

That's where we are at. It is around symptoms that everything we can have an idea about – as they say, as if the word had any meaning anymore – revolves. Symptoms orient you, all of you, such as you are. The only things that interest you – that don't fall flat and are not simply inane qua information – are the things that assume the appearance of symptoms – in other words, in theory, things that attract your attention [or: that make a sign to you, *qui vous font signe*] but which you don't understand in the least. This is the only sure thing: there are things that grab your attention, about which you understand nothing.

I will tell you how a Chinese word for "man" – it's actually untranslatable, that's the way it is, it means a "good guy" – does very odd little juggling tricks and switches back and forth between *xing* and *ming*. It is obviously too complicated for me to talk about today, but I am placing it on the horizon, at the cusp, in order to tell you that this is where we are heading. For, in any case, *xing* is something that doesn't work properly, something that is underdeveloped. We must figure out where to situate it.

There is something not very satisfying about the fact that *xing* can mean "nature," given the current state of natural history. There is no way we can find *xing* in the highly sophisticated thing we have to grasp or zero in on known as "surplus jouissance." It's so slippery that it isn't easy to put our finger on. It is certainly not what I am referring to when I talk about underdevelopment. 53

I realize that by ending now, because it is getting rather late, I will perhaps leave you with bated breath. I will nevertheless come back to it, in connection with the topic of metaphorical action [*agir*].

Since linguistics was my main focus today, I will say – assuming that linguistics be appropriately filtered, critiqued, and focused, and, in short, that we do whatever we want with what linguists do – why not take advantage of it, good Lord? They might just so happen to do something worthwhile.

If linguistics is what I said it was earlier, a metaphor constructed expressly in order not to work, that might give you an idea as to what our goal might be – where we stand with Mencius and a few others at his time who knew what they were saying.

Yet we must not confuse underdevelopment with the return to an archaic state. It is not because Mencius lived in the third century before Christ that I am claiming he represents some sort of primitive mentality. I am presenting him to you as someone who, in what he said, probably knew some of the things that we *don't* know when we say the same thing. This is what can allow us to learn with him to champion [*soutenir*] a metaphor that is not constructed so as not to work, but whose action we put in abeyance. I will, perhaps, try to show you the necessary pathway to it.

I will leave it there today as regards a discourse that might not be mere semblance.

February 10, 1971

IV

WRITING AND TRUTH

Richards' *Mencius on the Mind*
Writing is *not* language
The phallus as an instrument
Peirce's schema
Lorenzen's *Métamathématique*

Here is the name of the author of the little formulation [running down the left-hand side of this page]:

孟

子

Mengzi

This line was written by Mengzi around 250 B.C., in Chinese, as you can see, and can be found in Chapter 2 of Book IV, part two. (His work is sometimes organized differently, and in that case, it's in Part VIII of Book IV, part two, paragraph 26.) The Jesuits called him Mencius; they went to China well before there were sinologues. The latter first appeared toward the beginning of the nineteenth century, not before.

I was lucky enough to purchase the first book in which you can find Chinese characters juxtaposed with our own writing. It is a Chinese translation of Aesop's fables. It came out in 1840, and it boasts, rightly

性
也
則
故
而
已
矣
故
者

On the board

孟
子
曰
天
下
之
言

56

so, that it is the first book that provided such a translation on facing pages. That is not quite the same thing as the first book in which you can find both Chinese and European characters.

Take note that 1840 is approximately when sinologues first appeared. Jesuits had been in China for a long time, as some of you may recall. They almost managed to get China to fall in line with their goal as missionaries. Yet they allowed themselves to be a bit impressed by Chinese rites, and, as you may know, that gave them some trouble with Rome in the eighteenth century. Rome did not evince especially astute policies on that occasion, which sometimes happens.

In any case, in Voltaire's work – assuming you read Voltaire, and, of course, no one does anymore, which is dumb as it contains plenty of things – there is an appendix in *The Age of Louis XIV* which is, I believe, a lampoon that goes into the "war of the rites" [*Querelle des rites*] in great detail. The roots of many historical events can be traced back to it.

Whatever the case may be, we are talking about Mencius, and he wrote what I put up on the blackboard. As it is not strictly speaking part of my discourse today, I am fitting it in before my usual start time, which is 12:30 on the nose.

I am going to tell you, or, rather, I'm going to try to convey to you, what it means, and that will prime the pump concerning the topic I wish to address today – namely, the function of writing in our field.

1

Writing has existed in China since time immemorial.

By which I mean that, well before we have what are strictly speaking written works, writing already existed for ages. We cannot gauge how long it existed. Writing in China played an altogether pivotal role in a certain number of things that happened, and it enlightens us regarding what we might think of the function of writing.

It is clear that writing played an altogether decisive role in maintaining something specific to which we have access, having access to nothing else – namely, a type of social structure that held together for a very long time. Up until a recent era, one could have concluded that what held together in China had a totally different filiation than what arose among us, and specifically by one of the phyla that turns out to especially interest us – namely, the phylum of philosophy insofar as it is crucial for understanding the master's discourse, as I pointed out last year.

天
下
之
言
性
也

This is the opening line of his chapter. As I already showed on the blackboard last time, this character, 天, means sky, and is pronounced *tian*. *Tian xia*, 天下, means under the sky, everything that is under heaven. Here, in the third position, is a determinative, *zhi*, 之; it concerns something that is under heaven. What is under heaven? That is what comes next. What you see here, 言, is nothing but the designation of speech, which, in this case, is pronounced *yan*. *Yan xing*, 言 性 – I already put these characters up on the board last time and told you that *xing* is one of the elements that will preoccupy us this year, inasmuch as the term that comes closest to it is "nature." Lastly, *ye*, 也, is something that concludes a sentence, but without, strictly speaking, saying that it involves something along the lines of what we pronounce "is," "being." It is a conclusion, or, rather, a punctuation mark. For the sentence continues here, since things are written from right to left, with a certain *ze*, 則, which means "consequently," or which, in any case, indicates the consequent.

Let us thus consider what is at stake here. *Yan*, 言, means nothing other than language, but like all terms in Chinese, it can also be employed as a verb. Thus it can mean both "speech," and "what speaks." What does it speak? That would, in this case, be what follows – namely, *xing*, nature: "what speaks about nature under heaven," and *ye* would be a punctuation mark.

Nevertheless, and this is what makes it interesting to examine the way a sentence is written, we see that we could divide things up differently. We could say "speech," or even "language," because had he been trying to specifically indicate speech, he would have included a slightly different character. The way it is written here, the character can just as easily mean speech as language. These kinds of ambiguities are altogether fundamental in the use of what is written, and they constitute the import of what I write. As I pointed out to you at the beginning of my discourse this year, and especially last time, language takes on its import quite precisely insofar as the reference, as regards everything involving language, is always indirect.

We could thus also say that, insofar as it is in the world, insofar as it is under heaven, language is what constitutes *xing*, nature. Indeed, Mencius isn't talking about just any old nature, but rather the nature of speaking beings. In another passage, he specifies that, between human nature and animal nature, there is a difference which he indicates using two terms that clearly mean what they mean: "an infinite difference." That is, perhaps, the one that is defined here. As you will see, whether we adopt one or the other of these interpretations, the axis of what will be said to be the consequent will be the same.

gu

ze

Ze is therefore the consequence. *Ze gu* means "thus" [literally, "as a consequence of the cause"], for *gu* means nothing other than cause.

59   A book entitled *Mencius on the Mind* was committed to paper by a guy named Richards, who certainly was no lightweight. Richards and Ogden were the two leaders of a movement known as logical positivism, which was born in England at the beginning of the century and was altogether in sync with the best British philosophical tradition.

Their major work is entitled *The Meaning of Meaning*. I alluded to it in my *Écrits*, with a certain disparaging tone [p. 224]. Logical positivists stipulate that a text must have a graspable meaning, which leads them to devalue a certain number of philosophical statements owing to the fact that they do not provide any graspable meaning. In other words, as soon as a philosophical text is deemed to make no sense, it is immediately disqualified. It is only too clear that this is a way of eliminating things that does not allow us to get our bearings in any manner. For, if we begin from the principle that something that has no meaning cannot be essential to the development of a discourse, we quite simply lose the thread.

I am not, of course, saying that such a stipulation is not one way of proceeding, but that this way of proceeding – which prohibits any and every articulation whose meaning is not graspable – leads, for example, to the following: that we can no longer make use of mathematical discourse which, as the most qualified logicians have admitted, is characterized by the fact that we cannot attribute any meaning to it at one or another of its points. This does not stop it from being the most rigorously developed discourse there is.

We thus find ourselves at a point that must be brought out concerning the function of writing.

It is therefore *gu*, the cause, that is at issue, and insofar as *yi wei*, 以為. I already told you that *wei* can, in certain cases, mean "to act" [or: "action," *agir*], or even something along the lines of "doing" 60 [or: "making," *faire*], although it is not just any old kind of doing. The character *yi* here means something like "with." It is "with" that we proceed. How? As *li*, 利 – that is the word I am pointing to here. It means "gain," "interest," or "profit," and this is all the more remarkable if we look at the first chapter of Mencius's book.

Mencius presented himself to a certain prince, it doesn't matter which, of what constituted the kingdoms that were later known as the "combative kingdoms." The prince asked for his advice, and Mencius told him that he wasn't there to teach him the law that everyone was then following – namely, what will increase the kingdom's wealth, and in particular what we would call "surplus value." If there is a meaning that one can retroactively attribute to *li*, it is certainly that.

It is remarkable to see that what Mencius points out here is that, on the basis of the speech that is nature – or, if you will, on the basis of the speech that concerns nature – the point is to arrive at the cause, insofar as the said cause is *li*. *Gu er*, 故 而, means both "and" and "but." *Er yi yi*, 而 已 矣, means "it's simply that." And so that there can be no doubt about it, the *yi*, 矣, that ends it here is a conclusive *yi*, and has the same accent as "only" [or: solely]. It is *yi*, 矣, and that is enough. It is here that I will, in short, allow myself to recognize that, as regards the effects of discourse – as regards, what is under heaven – what comes out of this is no other than the function of the cause insofar as it is surplus jouissance.

There are two ways you can find this text by Mencius. Either you get yourself the French edition (which is, in fact, a very fine one) that was published at the end of the nineteenth century by a Jesuit by the name of Séraphin Couvreur: *Les Quatre Livres* ["The Four Books" of Confucianism, 1895]. Or you can order *Mencius on the Mind* by Richards, which was published by Kegan Paul in London. I don't know if there are many copies that are still "available,"* as they say. But for those of you who are curious to have a look at something that sheds considerable light on a reflection on language, which is the work of a neo-positivist who is certainly not negligible, it is worth purchasing. Those willing to make the effort to get hold of a copy, but who are unable to, might be able to have a photocopy of it made for them. That will allow them to perhaps better understand what I will extract from it this year, for I will come back to it.

61   It is, thus, one thing to talk about the origin of language, and
another to talk about its connection with what I teach, in accordance with what I articulated last year as the analyst's discourse.

As you know, linguistics began with Humboldt's prohibition
against speculating about the origin of language, failing which one
goes astray. It is rather significant that someone, right smack in the
middle of the era of mythmaking about how things arose – which,
in fact, typified the style of the beginning of the nineteenth century –
posited that nothing would ever be situated, founded, or articulated
regarding language if one did not begin by prohibiting questions of
origin.

It is an example that should have been followed elsewhere, for
that would have spared us copious harebrained lucubrations of a
kind that we could call "primitivist." There's nothing like referring
to the "primitive" to primitivize thought.

The more thought claims that what it discovers is "primitive," the
more thought itself regresses.

2

$$\frac{a}{S_2} \quad \frac{\$}{S_1}$$

I must tell you, since, in short, you didn't hear [or: understand,
entendu] it: the analyst's discourse is nothing other than the logic of
action.

Why didn't you hear it? Because what I articulated last year, with
these little letters on the blackboard – with little a over S_2, and then
what we find at the level of the analysand, namely, the function of
the subject qua barred, $\$$, and qua what he produces, S_1 (which are
signifiers, and not just any old signifiers: master signifiers) – was
written. You didn't hear it because it was written – and written
exactly like this, for I wrote it on the board many times.

That is what makes writing different from speech; speech has to
be added back into it; in order to be understood, writing has to be
seriously layered over [or: coated (or blanketed)] with speech – but,
naturally, that cannot occur without theoretical inconveniences.

62   You can write tons of things without anyone hearing them. They're
written all the same. That's even why I entitled my *Écrits* as I did.
That scandalized sensitive people, and not just any old people. It
is truly odd that the person who was literally convulsed by it was
a Japanese woman. I will comment on that later. The title didn't
convulse anyone in France, naturally, and the Japanese woman I

am speaking about is not here today. Anyone from that tradition would, I think, know why such an insurrection occurred in her case.

It is via speech, of course, that a pathway toward writing is paved. If I entitled my *Écrits* as I did, it's because it represented an attempt, an attempt at writing; this is sufficiently indicated by the fact that it gave rise to graphs. The problem is that people who profess to comment on my work start immediately in on the graphs. They are wrong: the graphs are comprehensible only as a function, I would say, of the least stylistic effect of my *Écrits*, writings that are, in a sense, stairs that allow access to the graphs. Otherwise, what is written, taken all by itself – whether we are talking about this or that schema, the one known as L or any other one, even the complete graph of desire itself – is open to all sorts of misunderstandings.

What is at stake is speech [*une parole*] insofar as it tries to pave the way to these graphs. We must not forget this speech, because it is the very same speech that is reflected in the fundamental rule of psychoanalysis, which is, as you know: talk, talk, wager that it's enough for you to blather; that's the box out of which all of language's gifts flow – it's Pandora's box. How is this connected to the graphs? Naturally, no one has dared go so far as to say that the graphs allow in any way for a return to the origin of language. If there's one thing that we see in them immediately, it is that they not only don't deliver that, they don't even promise it.

Today we are going to talk about the relationship to truth that results from what is known as free association – in other words, the free exercise of speech. I have never spoken about it without irony. We can no more call association free than we can say that a bound variable [or: dependent variable, *variable liée*] in a mathematical function is free. The function defined by analytic discourse obviously isn't free, it is bound. It is bound by the conditions that I will quickly designate as those of the analytic consulting room.

How far is my analytic discourse, such as it is defined here by this writing, from the analytic consulting room? This is precisely what constitutes what I will call my dissent regarding a certain number of analytic consulting rooms. Moreover, this definition of analytic discourse, in order to indicate where I stand, doesn't seem to those who work in those analytic consulting rooms to correspond to their (pre)conditions. Now, what my discourse traces out, or at least delivers up, are some of the (pre)conditions of the analytic consulting room. To gauge what one does when one enters into an analysis is clearly of importance, and in any case, as for me, this is indicated by the fact that I always ensure that there are numerous preliminary meetings.

A pious person, who I will not designate in any other way, apparently thought – according to what I most recently heard, and this dates back three months – that it was an untenable wager on my part to base transference on the subject-supposed-to-know, since the method requires the analyst to maintain a total absence of biases regarding the case at hand. The subject-supposed-to-know what, then? I will allow myself to raise the question to this person. Must the psychoanalyst be assumed to know what he is doing, and does he in fact know what he is doing?

This will allow you to understand why I raise questions about transference as I do in "The Direction of the Treatment," for example. I am delighted to see that people at my *École* study that text. Something new is happening, which is that people at my *École* have begun to work together as a school. That is new enough to be worth highlighting. I was pleased to observe that people noticed that I don't in any way say exactly what transference is in that text. It is very precisely by proffering the "subject-supposed-to-know," such as I define it, that the question whether the analyst can be assumed to know what he is doing remains open.

si

This is a little Chinese character. I'm sorry that the chalk does not allow me to include the details that a brush allows for. This character has a meaning, satisfying the stipulations of the logical positivists, a meaning which, as you will see, is quite ambiguous, since it means both "crafty" and "personal," in the sense of "private." It has a few other meanings as well. But what strikes me as remarkable is its written form, for it will immediately allow me to tell you where to situate the terms around which my discourse will revolve today.

If we situate somewhere, let's say at the top [number 1 in Figure 4.1], what I call the effects of language, in the broadest sense – you will see that it is broad, I have no need, it seems to me, to underscore this – it is here, at the intersection [number 2 in Figure 4.1], that we will have to place the source of their power. It is at that source that analytic discourse reveals something, that it takes a step forward, as I try to remind you, even though we are talking about first truths in psychoanalysis. It is there that I am immediately going to begin. We thus have here, on the horizontal line [number 3 in Figure 4.1], the fact of writing [or: what is written, *le fait de l'écrit*].

Figure 4.1 The Chinese Character *si*

It is very important in our era – owing to certain statements that have been made which tend to generate highly regrettable confusions – to recall that writing is not first, but rather second, with respect to any and every functioning of language. We must also recall that, without writing, it is nevertheless impossible to question anew what results first and foremost from the effect of language as such – in other words, from the symbolic order, that is, the dimension (I'm saying that to please you, but you know that I introduced another term, "demansion," the residence or locus) of truth as Other.

I've heard that this term "demansion" raised questions in some of your minds. Well, if "demansion" is, in fact, a new term that I coined, and if it doesn't yet have a meaning, then it is up to you to give it one. Questioning the demansion of truth in its dwelling place is something – that is what is new in what I am presenting today – that can only be done via writing, insofar as logic is constituted solely on the basis of writing.

This is what I am introducing at this point in my discourse this year: there can be no logical questioning except on the basis of writing, insofar as writing is *not* language. That is why I stated that there is no such thing as a metalanguage. Writing, even insofar as it is distinguished from language, is there to show us that, whereas it is owing to writing that language can be questioned, this is true precisely because writing is not language, but can only be constructed or manufactured on the basis of its reference to language. 65

3

Having posited that – something which has the advantage of conveying my aim or design – I will turn to something that concerns the point related to the surprise by which the effect of looping back (by which I tried to define the junction between truth and knowledge [see, for example, Chapter II of this Seminar]) is signaled, and which I stated in the following terms: there is no such thing as a sexual relationship [*rapport sexuel*] in speaking beings.

There is a first condition that can allow us to see this immediately: it is that the relationship between the sexes [*rapport sexuel*], like any other relationship, subsists, in the final analysis, only on the basis of writing.

The crux of a relationship is an "application" [or: law of correspondence (or mapping), *application*] – *a* applied to *b*:

$$a \rightarrow b$$

If you don't write it *a* and *b*, you don't have the relationship itself. That doesn't mean things don't occur in reality. But why, then, would you call it a relationship? This colossal fact would already suffice to render, let us say, conceivable that there's no such thing as a sexual relationship, but would in no wise determine whether one can or cannot manage to write it. I would go even further: there is something that people have been doing, for a long time already, which is to write it by using little planetary signs – namely, the relationship between what is male and what is female:

I would even say that, thanks to the progress that microscopes have allowed (don't forget that prior to Swammerdam we could have no idea about this), it has seemed for a while now that –
66 however meiotic the process may be by which so-called gonadal cells provide a model of fertilization from which reproduction stems – something is, in fact, grounded there that allows us to situate the relationship between the sexes, however complex it may be, at a level said to be biological.

What is certainly strange – but, good Lord, not so strange, after all, but I would like to evoke its dimension of strangeness – is that the model for the duality and adequacy of this relationship has always been what I mentioned to you last time: these little Chinese signs. I suddenly grew impatient when drawing them for you last week, as if I were doing so just to impress you. This one is the *yin* that I didn't write for you last time, and this one is *yang*, as you saw last time; you have to add another little line over here.

Yin and *yang*, the male and female principles, are hardly specific to the Chinese tradition, for you find them in every sort of cogitation about the relationships of action and passion, about form and substance, and about *Purusha*, mind, and *Prakriti*, some sort of feminized matter. The general model of this male to female relationship is clearly what has long haunted attempts to situate speaking beings with respect to the forces in the world, those that are *tian xia*, under heaven.

tian

xia

It is worth highlighting something that is altogether new, which I called the effect of surprise, and to understand what came out of analytic discourse, whatever it is worth. It is that it is untenable to consider this duality the slightest bit adequate. 67

The so-called function of the phallus – which is, in truth, very clumsily handled, but which is there and functions in our experience, and is not simply tied to something that should be considered deviant or pathological, but is essential to the establishment of analytic discourse – renders sexual bipolarity untenable, untenable in a way that literally vaporizes what might be written about this relationship [or: vaporizes whatever aspect of this relationship can be written, *ce qui peut s'écrire de ce rapport*].

We must distinguish the intrusion of the phallus from what some people thought they could translate using the term "lack of a signifier" [see Chapter II of this Seminar]. It is not the lack of a signifier that is at stake, but the obstacle to a relationship.

In placing the emphasis on an organ, the phallus in no way designates the penis as an organ with its specific physiology, nor even the function that one can, my word, plausibly attribute to it – that of copulation. When you look at psychoanalytic texts, the term "phallus" unambiguously concerns its relationship to jouissance. It is in that respect that those texts distinguish it from the physiological function.

There is – and this is what is posited as constituting the phallus's function – a jouissance that constitutes something in this relationship, that is different from the relationship between the sexes. What is that something? It is what I will call its "truth condition."

The angle from which the organ is viewed, with regard to the set of living beings, is in no way linked to this particular form. If you knew the variety of copulatory organs that exist among insects, you might easily be shocked – shock is, after all, a principle that is always helpful in investigating reality – that this is how things work among the vertebrates.

I must move on quickly here, for I will not repeat everything and draw it all out at length. Have a look at the text that I mentioned earlier, "The Direction of the Treatment and the Principles of Its Power." The phallus is the organ insofar as it *is*, that's *i.s.* – we're talking about being – insofar as it is feminine jouissance.

68   Therein lies the incompatibility between being and having. I repeated that in the text a number of times, adding certain stylistic accents – which, let me repeat, are just as important for making headway as are the graphs to which they lead. At the notorious Congress in Royaumont where I gave that paper, a few people snickered at me. If that's the whole story – if being and having are all it's about – that seemed not to be of very great scope to them; you just pick one, being or having. That is, nevertheless, what is known as castration.

What I propose to posit is that language – I placed it here at the top [number 1 in Figure 4.1] – has its dedicated field in the gap [number 2 in Figure 4.1] in the relationship between the sexes, such as it is left open by the phallus. What it introduces here is not two terms that are defined as male and female, but a choice between terms whose nature and function are very different: being and having.

What proves this, corroborates it, and renders this distance absolutely obvious and definitive is the substitution of what is known as the sexual law for the relationship between the sexes; it seems that people didn't notice the substitution. Therein lies the distance in which we see that the following two things have nothing in common: what one can state, on the one hand, about a relationship that would lay down the law – insofar as it has to do, in any form whatsoever, with "application" [or: mapping; see *a—>b* earlier], functions in mathematics illustrating it as precisely as possible – and a law, on the other hand, that is coherent with the whole register of what is known as desire and what is known as prohibition. The conjunction – nay the identity, as I dared put it – of desire and law has to do with the very gap wrought by this inscribed prohibition. Correlatively, everything that pertains to the effect of language, everything that instates the "demansion" of truth, is posited on the basis of a fictional structure.

Regarding the correlation that has always existed between rituals and myths, it is ridiculously flimsy to say that myths are simply commentaries on rituals – in other words, things that are created to prop them up and explain them. And in accordance with a topology – one I have been employing for long enough not to have to recall it to mind here – rituals and myths are like two sides of the same coin, on the condition that the two sides be continuous, as in a Möbius strip. What does it mean that in psychoanalytic discourse we continue to use the residual myth known as the Oedipal myth, God only knows why, when, in fact, it is in *Totem and Taboo* that we find the myth, of Freud's own invention, of the primal father insofar as he enjoys all the women? That is what we should investigate using something 69 that goes further: logic and writing.

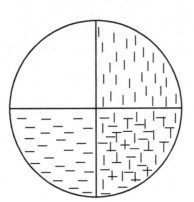

Figure 4.2 Peirce's Schema

I presented Charles Sanders Peirce's schema here a long time ago [see Seminar IX] in relation to propositions, there being four types of them: universals, particulars, affirmatives, and negatives.

If Peirce's schema is of interest, it is because it shows that if we say that every *x* is *y*, that every something has a specific attribute, it is a perfectly acceptable universal proposition even if there aren't any *x*'s.

Let me remind you that in Peirce's little schema, we have here, in the upper right-hand quadrant, a certain number of lines that are all vertical. In the lower left-hand corner, we have no vertical lines; all the lines are horizontal. In the lower right-hand quadrant, we have a mixture of vertical and horizontal lines. Lastly, in the upper left-hand corner, there are no lines whatsoever. The specificity of each proposition derives from taking two adjacent quadrants together. By joining the two upper quadrants, one can say that every line is vertical. If it is not vertical, that implies that there are no lines. As for the negative, we take the two quadrants on the left: either there are no lines, or else there are no vertical lines.

What is designated by the myth of the enjoyment of all women by the father of the primal horde is that there is no such thing as "all women." Nothing universal can be said about women. This is what results from a questioning of the phallus, not from a questioning of the relationship between the sexes as regards the jouissance that the phallus constitutes, since I said that it was feminine jouissance.

These statements require us to radically alter a certain number of perspectives.

After all, it might be possible for there to be knowledge of the jouissance that we call sexual that a "certain woman" has. That is not unthinkable; there are some mythical traces of it in different places. What are known as the *Tantra* are supposedly practiced. It is clear, nevertheless, that the skill of flutists has long been far more conspicuous, if you allow me to put it thusly. I am not saying this in order to be obscene; I assume that there is at least one person here who knows what it means to play the flute.

Someone recently pointed out to me, regarding flute-playing – but one can say the same thing about the use of any instrument – the division of the body made necessary by the use of an instrument, whatever it may be. I mean the break in synergy. It suffices to use any sort of instrument. Get on a pair of skis and you will immediately see that your synergies must be broken. Pick up a golf club – I've done so lately, I started playing again – it's the same. There are two different types of movement that you must perform at the same time; at the outset, you absolutely cannot manage to do so, because they don't go together. The person who reminded me of this regarding the flute also pointed out that, when it comes to singing, where, apparently there is no instrument – that's what makes singing especially interesting – you still have to divide your body. You divide two things that are altogether distinct, but which are usually absolutely synergistic – namely, the smooth flow of the voice [or: poised creation of sound, *la pose de la voix*] and breathing.

Fine. Now these first truths – which I didn't have to be reminded of, since as I told you, I had a recent experience with a golf club – leave open the question whether knowledge about the phallic instrument can still be found somewhere.

But the phallic instrument is unlike any other instrument. I already told you that the phallic instrument must not be confused with the penis, just as in singing [the smooth flow of the voice must not be confused with breathing]. The penis takes its cue from [or: targets (or is regulated by), *se règle sur*] the law – in other words, from desire; in other words, from surplus jouissance; in other words, from the cause of desire; in other words, from fantasy. And there, the supposed knowledge of a woman who knows encounters a bone(r) [figuratively, a hitch, *os*] – the exact one that is lacking in the

70

organ, if you will allow me to continue in the same vein, because in certain animals, there is a bone, it's true! Here it is lacking, there's a bone missing. That is not the phallus; it is desire and its functioning. Consequently, nothing attests to a woman's insertion into the law, 71 to what makes up for the sexual relationship, except for the man's desire.

It is enough to have a tiny bit of experience with psychoanalysis to be convinced of this. Man's desire, as I just said, is linked to its cause, which is surplus jouissance. Or, as I have put it many times before, it finds its source in the field from which everything, every linguistic effect, begins – in other words, in the Other's desire. We realize that, in this case, Woman is the Other. Except that she is an Other of a totally different type [or: jurisdiction, *ressort*], a totally different register than her knowledge, whatever it may be.

Thus we have the phallic instrument posited as the cause, in quotes, of language – I did not say "origin." And despite the fact that it is, good Lord, getting late, I will quickly point out the trace of this we can have by continuing, whether we like it or not, to prohibit four-letter words.

I know that there are people who are waiting for me to do what I promised, to allude to *Éden, Éden, Éden* [a novel by Pierre Guyotat, published in 1970] and to say why I don't sign – what are those things called? – petitions about such matters.

It is certainly not that I have scant esteem for what he tried to do. In its own way, it is comparable to my *Écrits*. Except that it is far more hopeless. It is entirely hopeless to "language" the phallic instrument. And it is because I consider it hopeless to do so that I also think it can give rise to nothing but misunderstanding.

You can see that my refusal to sign a petition about it is situated, in this case, at a highly theoretical level.

4

Where I would like to go with this is the following: from whence do we investigate truth?

For truth can say whatever it likes. It is an oracle. Oracles have always existed, and after they speak one just has to make do.

Except that there is something new, isn't there? The first new fact – since oracles have existed, in other words, since time immemorial – is that in one of my writings, entitled "The Freudian Thing," I indicated something that no one had ever said, had they? (But since it was written, naturally you didn't hear it.) I said that truth speaks I ["I, truth, speak," *Écrits*, p. 340].

72   If you had given its proper weight to the kind of polemical luxuri-
ance I provided in order to present truth in that way – I don't even
recall what I wrote, something like "entering into the room, with a
big smashing of mirrors" – that might have opened up your ears.
The sound of mirrors breaking doesn't strike you in a written text.
And yet it is rather well written – that is what I referred to earlier as
a "stylistic effect." It would certainly have helped you understand
what it means to say "truth speaks I."
    It means that you can say "you" to it, and I will tell you what
purpose that serves.
    You'll naturally presume that I'm going to tell you that it
serves the purpose of generating dialogue. I've been saying for
a long time that there's no such thing as dialogue. And still less
with truth, naturally. Nevertheless, if you read something entitled
Métamathématique by Lorenzen (I brought it with me today, it
was published by Gauthier-Villars and Mouton [in Paris in 1967,
translated from German], and I'm even going to tell you on what
page you will find some very astute things), you will find dialogues,
written dialogues – meaning that the same guy wrote both parts. On
page 22, you'll find a quite peculiar, but very instructive dialogue. It
is highly instructive and I could translate it in more than one way,
including by using my "being" and "having" from earlier today.
    But I will simply remind you of something that I have already
stressed – namely, that none of the supposed paradoxes that classical logic gets bent out of shape about, for example, that of "I am
lying," hold up unless they are written.
    It is absolutely clear that to say "I am lying" is something that
poses no obstacle, given that people lie all the time – so why not say
so? What does this mean? That it is only when it is written that there
is a paradox, because then a question arises: "Are you lying now or
are you telling the truth?" It's exactly the same thing that I pointed
out to you when I asked you to "write the smallest number that can
be written in more than fifteen words." You don't see any obstacle
in that. Yet if it is written, you count the words and you realize that
they were only thirteen in what I just said. But you don't count them
unless they're written down.
    I defy you to count them if they're spoken in Japanese, because
in Japanese you have to wonder what constitutes a word. There are
little whimpers, little *o*'s and little *wa*'s, that you wonder whether
73 you should attach to the word or detach and count as separate
words. They're not even words; they're "uh"! That's the way it is.
But when things are written out, words become countable.
    So you will perceive that regarding truth, just as in Lorenzen's
Métamathématique, if you posit that one cannot say both "yes" and

"no" about the same point, you win. You will see later what you win. But if you wager that it is either "yes" or "no," then you lose. Take a look at Lorenzen, but I will illustrate it for you immediately.

I posit the following: "It is not true," I say to truth, "that you speak truly and that you lie at the same time." Truth may respond in a wide variety of ways, since you're the one who is putting words in its mouth, so it costs you nothing. In any case, it will lead to the same result; but I will spell it out for you in order to follow Lorenzen's lead. The truth says "I am speaking truly," and you respond, "You said it!" [or: "Tell me about it!," *Je ne te le fais pas dire!*]. So, in order to bust your chops, truth says, "I am lying." To which you respond, "Now I've won, I know that you are contradicting yourself."

This is exactly what the unconscious shows us; it has no greater scope. It is perfectly acceptable to the unconscious to always speak the truth and to lie. It's up to you to know that. What does that teach you? That you only know something about truth when it is unleashed [*elle se déchaîne*]. Here it has been unleashed, broken your chain, and told you both things when you'd said that their conjunction was not tenable.

But let us assume you said the contrary: "Either you are speaking truly or you are lying." That is going to cost you big-time. What does the truth reply? "I'll grant you that, and I'll willingly put on a leash [or: limit myself, *je m'enchaîne*]. You tell me, 'Either you are speaking truly or you are lying,' and, indeed, that is quite true." But here you don't know anything about what it told you, since either it is speaking truly or else it is lying – such that you lose.

I don't know if you can see the relevance of this, but it means something that we constantly experience. If truth refuses to cooperate [or: doesn't go along (or play ball), *se refuse*], then it can serve some purpose for me. We deal with that all the time in analysis. If it gives in [*s'abandonne*] and accepts the leash, whatever it may be – well, then I don't understand anything anymore. In other words, it leaves me something to be desired. It leaves me something to be desired, and it leaves me in my position as a petitioner, because I am mistaken in thinking that I can deal with a truth that I can only recognize when it is unleashed. You show what kind of garbage [*déchet-nement*, a play on *déchet*, scrap or garbage, and *déchaînement*, unleashing] you are made of.

There is something worth highlighting in this relationship, which is the function of something I have slowly been putting in the hot seat for a long time, and which is known as freedom. It just so happens that by fantasizing, there are some who come up with harebrained ideas about how, if not truth itself, at least the phallus could be domesticated. I won't go into the wide variety of details that these sorts of lucubrations can go into. But there's something very striking there. Apart from a sort of lack of seriousness – which is, perhaps, the defining characteristic of perversion – in these elegant solutions, it is clear that people for whom this little business is serious,

> – because, good Lord, language matters to them, as does writing, if only because it allows for logical investigation, because in the end, what is logic if not the absolutely fabulous paradox allowed only by writing, which is to make truth into a referent. That is obviously how they begin, when they give the first formulas of propositional logic. They take as their point of reference that there are propositions that can be noted "true" and others that can be noted "false." The reference to truth begins with that. To refer to truth is to posit the absolutely false, that is, a false to which one can refer as such. I'll return now to what I was saying –

serious people, who come up with elegant solutions that would entail the domestication of the phallus, well, it's odd – they are the ones who refuse to cooperate [*se refusent*]. Why? In order to preserve what is known as freedom, insofar as it is precisely identical to the nonexistence of the sexual relationship.

Need I indicate that the relationship between man and woman, insofar as it is radically skewed [*faussé*] by the law, the so-called sexual law, allows us to desire [or: leaves something to be desired when it comes to the idea] that each of us will have the partner that suits him? If that happens, what will we say? Certainly not that it was quite natural, since there is no nature in that regard, since Woman doesn't exist. It is a woman's dream that She exist, and it is the dream that gave rise to Don Juan. If there was a man for whom Woman existed, it would be marvelous, you could be sure of his desire. It is a woman's hairbrained lucubration. When a man finds *his* woman, what can be said if not the romantic formulation: it was fated, it was written.

We find ourselves once again at the intersection, which is the one where I told you I would shift the status of the true lord, the type that is just a little bit above the ordinary, and that is translated, very badly I'm afraid, by "man."

xing   *ming*

The shift occurs between *xing*, nature – such as it is, owing to the effect of language, inscribed in the disjunction between man and woman – and *ming*, heaven's decree, this other character (which I have already once drawn for you on the board), meaning "it is written," the character freedom shrinks from.

February 17, 1971

V

WRITING AND SPEECH

L'achose and writing
Science and writing
Chinese and Japanese
The representation of words
"The Purloined Letter" revisited

Am I, am I present when I speak to you? The thing I talk to you about would have to be here for this to be the case. Now it suffices to say that the thing can only be written *l'achose* [a play on *la chose*, the thing, and *a-chose*, nonthing or object *a* thing], as I just wrote it on the blackboard, meaning that the thing is absent from the place it holds. Or, more precisely, that once it is taken away, little object *a*, which holds this place, leaves in it only the sexual act such as I emphasize it – in other words, castration.

I can only attest that *la, là n'a lyse*, if you will allow me [a play on *l'analyse* (analysis), meaning something like "that place has no lysis"], is nothing at all if it does not concern castration [*la castration*]. That's the word for it – *Oh là là!*

Philosophical chatter [*baratin*], which is not nothing – chatter churns [literally churns butter, *baratte*], and there's nothing wrong with that – served a purpose for a long time, but it has been tiring us out for a while now. It went so far as to produce *être-là* [literally "being (t)here"], which is sometimes more modestly translated into French as "presence," whether or not the word "living" is added to it – in short, what scholars call *Dasein*. I was delighted to come across the word in something I wrote (I'll tell you in which text it was in a little while), and in that way I realized with surprise that the formulation I provided for people who were a bit hard of hearing – "Eat your *Dasein*" – goes pretty far back. No matter. We'll return to that later.

Philosophical chatter is not totally incoherent. It incarnates that presence or "being (t)here" in a discourse that it initiates solely by disincarnating, by *épaché*, bracketing; that's what *épaché* means. It's better when it doesn't have exactly the same structure [as in French, *la mise entre parentheses* (putting into parentheses)] – in 78 other words, it's better in Greek. It makes it clear that the only way to be (t)here is to be bracketed. This brings us to the nub of what I want to tell you today.

If there is a hole at the level of *l'achose*, it allows you to already sense that this is a way of depicting the hole, and that it can be depicted in but one way. How? To take a truly trivial comparison, like retinal spots, which the eye has no interest in being encumbered with when, after looking at the sun, it then turns to the landscape. It doesn't see its "being (t)here" there – the eye isn't crazy. There's a whole slew of *Klein d'oeil* bottles [a play on Klein bottles and *clin d'oeil* (wink or reference to something)] for you. No philosophical chatter, for you sense that it merely fulfills its university function there, whose limits I tried to trace out for you last year, at the same time, moreover, as I traced out the limits of what you can do from within it, even if it is revolution.

To denounce the said presence as "logocentric," as has been done – the idea of inspired speech, as they say, in the name of the fact that we can, of course laugh at inspired speech, and chalk up to speech all the idiocy in which a certain discourse went astray, leading us toward a mythical "arche-writing," constituted only, in short, by what we rightly perceive to be a blind spot that can be pointed to in everything that has been said about writing – none of that gets us anywhere. People always talk about something else in order to speak about *l'achose*.

What I said way back when about "full speech" (one shouldn't overuse the term, I'm not full to the brim with talk about full speech, and I believe that the vast majority of you here have never heard me make anything of it) is that it *fulfills* – these are true linguistic finds and they are always quite pretty – the function of *l'achose* that is on the blackboard. In other words, speech always outstrips the speaker; the speaker is spoken; I have been saying that for quite a while now.

Where do we see this? That is what I'd like to indicate in my Seminar this year. Can you believe it? I am still at the stage of "I'd like to" after giving this Seminar for twenty years!

That's the way it is, naturally, because I didn't say it, after all. Yet it has been obvious for a long time. It has been obvious, first of all, because you are here in order for me to show it to you. But if what I say is true, your "being (t)here" is no more proof of that than mine 79 is. What I have been showing [*montre*] you for quite a while does not suffice for you to see it. I have to demonstrate [*démontre*] it.

To demonstrate, in this case, is to say what I was showing. It wasn't just any old thing, of course, but I didn't show you *l'achose*. Why not? Because it can't be shown; it has to be demonstrated.

I could, thus, draw your attention to things that I was showing, insofar as you didn't see what they could demonstrate.

To show my hand regarding my topic today, I will call it writing, with all the ambiguity that may entail.

1

You can't exactly say that I have burdened you with an onslaught of writings.

The ones I put together one fine day, feeling totally unable to make myself understood by psychoanalysts – I mean, even those who remained aggregated [*agrégés*] like that, because they hadn't been able to sail off to other shores – really had to be wrenched from my hands. In the end, I realized that there were so many other people who were interested in what I was saying – a little beginning of absent "being (t)here" – that I let go of my *Écrits*. And then, good gracious, they were consumed in a far vaster circle than the one you comprise, if I can believe the sales figures my publisher sends me.

It is a funny phenomenon, and it's worth dwelling on for a moment, insofar as, to stick with what I am always doing, my discourse revolved very precisely around an experience – an experience which is perfectly locatable, and which, in any case, I strove to articulate, especially last year, by trying to situate the structure of the analyst's discourse.

It is thus owing to my design – which in no way claims to provide a worldview, but simply to say what it seems self-evident one can say to analysts – that I gave a course for ten years in a rather well-known place, Sainte-Anne Hospital, that certainly did not claim to use writing except in a very precise way, which is the one that I will try to define today.

Those who were here at that time cannot dispute this. There aren't many of them left here today, of course, but a few nevertheless. There must be a handful of you who were here the first few months, and they can attest to what I did. I patiently, painstakingly, slowly, politely, and obsequiously constructed things called graphs for my audience piece by piece and step by step. A few such graphs are still floating around and you can easily find them. Thanks to the work of Jacques-Alain Miller, to whose devotion I pay homage, and whom I allowed to create a classified index of his own conception, you can easily see on what pages the graphs are found in *Écrits*. That will spare you the effort of searching through it yourself.

By doing so, you can already notice that there are things that are not like the rest of the printed text. The graphs you find there are not, of course, without presenting a little difficulty. Of what sort? Of interpretation, of course. You should realize that they were clear as day to the people for whom I constructed them. Before indicating the direction of a line, its intersection with another line, or the little letter found at that intersection, I talked for half an hour or three-quarters of an hour to justify what I was doing.

I am belaboring this, not to pat myself on the back – in the end, I enjoyed doing it, and no one was asking me to do it, quite the contrary – but because, with it, we enter into the heart of what we can say about what is written [*l'écrit*], nay about writing [*l'écriture*].

They are the same thing, after all. People speak about writing as if it were independent of the written, which sometimes makes discourse quite cumbersome. Moreover, the term "*ure*" that is added to *écrit* makes us realize what sort of funny *biture* [drunkenness or a length of rope or chain with which to moor a boat] is involved here. What is clear is that to talk about *l'achose* as it is there on the board, well, that should already in and of itself enlighten you regarding the fact that I had to take up as a "device" [*appareil*], that's all I'll say about it here, the prop of writing in the form of the graph.

The form the graph takes is worth considering. Take any of its versions, the last one for example, the big one, the one you find, I no longer know where it is, where it is floating. I think it is in "Subversion of the Subject and Dialectic of Desire" [*Écrits*, p. 692]. The thing is constructed as follows:

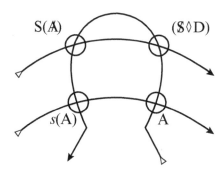

S(Ⱥ)   (\$◊D)

s(A)   A

Figure 5.1 Simplified Schema of the Graph of Desire

There are letters here, added in parentheses, barred S, lozenge, and capital D for demand, \$◊D, and here we have the S of the signifier, the promising [or: load-bearing, *porteur*] Signifier, qua function of barred A, S(A). You grasp that if writing can serve some purpose, it is insofar as it is different from speech – from speech that can lean on writing. Speech is not translated by S(A), for example. But while it does lean on it, if only on its form, speech must remember that this form does not exist without there being another line here that intersects the first one, and that is provided with intersection points s(A) and A itself.

I apologize for going into this, but, after all, some of you know this figure well enough that this reminder suffices, and the others can, good Lord, have a look at the page on which it is found. What is clear is that one cannot fail to feel at the very least solicited, let us say, by this figure, solicited to respond to the necessity of what it commands when you begin to interpret it.

Everything depends on the meaning you give A. There is one meaning proposed in the writing in which I just so happened to insert it. The meanings of the other mathemes are thus not free to deviate very much from that.

What is clear is something that must (at least I think so) have struck you as having been sufficiently spelled out since that time – namely, that this graph (this one, like all the others, and not simply mine) represents what is known as a "topology" in the highly developed language that was little by little provided by the logical investigation of mathematics. There can be no topology without writing. You have perhaps even noticed, if you've ever opened up Aristotle's *Analytics*, that we find in it a first sketch of a topology. It consists in making holes in writing. Take, for example, "All animals are mortal" – you erase "animals," and you erase "mortal," and you replace them with the pinnacle of writing: simple letters.   82

People say, and it is, perhaps, true, that this was facilitated by the Greeks' peculiar affinity for letters. We can't exactly say how. On the topic, you might have a look at some very engaging things James Février says, regarding some sort of artifice, jerry-rigging, and forcing that the invention of logic supposedly constituted with regard to what we can rather sanely call the norms of writing – the norms [*les normes*], not the enormous [*l'énorme* (a homonym)], although both are true. I would suggest in passing that it has something to do with Euclid.

I can merely toss that out in passing, since, after all, it has to be verified. I don't see why I wouldn't occasionally toss out a little suggestion, even to people who are very advanced in a certain field, that they will perhaps laugh at, because they realized it a long time ago. Indeed, it is hard to see why they wouldn't have noticed the fact that triangles – since triangles are the point of departure – are nothing other than writings, or things that are written. It is not because they defined "equal" as "metrically superimposable" that this runs counter to it. A triangle is a writing in which the metrically superimposable is "blatherable" [or: speakable, *jaspinable*]. It absolutely does not depend on the gap; it depends on you, the blatherer. However you write the triangle, even if you do it like this [Lacan draws on the blackboard], you demonstrate the nature of the isosceles triangle – namely, that if there are two equal sides, these two angles are equal. It's enough for you to have provided this little writing, because it is never much better than the isosceles triangle I just drew. It is said that the Greeks were gifted when it came to writing. Yet, that doesn't go very far.

We could perhaps go a bit further. For the time being, let us at least take note of the following: they realized very clearly what a postulate was. It has no other definition than the following: it is what – in the request one makes of one's interlocutor, that he not immediately say "get the hook" [or: "get him off stage," *crochet*] – is not, owing to the simple existence of the graph, forced upon discourse.

The Greeks thus seem to have known how to handle writing very astutely. They seem to have carried out a subtle reduction of what was already out there in the form of writing.

83   That was incredibly useful. It is altogether clear that there can be no empire, if you will grant me the word, or even the slightest empiricism, without the medium of writing.

2

If you will allow me to extrapolate from the same vein I am exploring, I will indicate to you the horizon or distant aim that is guiding all of this. Naturally, this can only be justified if the lines of perspective turn out to converge. What comes hereafter will show you that they do.

In the beginning, *en archè*, as they say – which has nothing to do with any sort of temporality, since temporality stems therefrom – in the beginning is speech [or: the word, *la parole*]. But there is, all the same, a good chance that speech did things during times that were not yet centuries. (They are centuries only for us, you see, thanks to radiant carbon [or: carbon dating], and a few other retroactive things like that, which take writing as their point of departure.) In short, for a bit of something that we might call, not time, but *aión* [Greek for eon], the *aión* of *aións*, as they say, people relished talking about things like that [e.g., "In the beginning . . ."]. They had their reasons for doing so, for they were closer to them than we are; speech did things that were surely less and less discernible from writing because they were its effects.

What does writing mean? We must home in on that a little. When we see what people commonly call writing, it is altogether clear and certain that it is something that, in a sense, has repercussions on speech.

Regarding the habitat of speech, I believe that I said enough things in the last few classes for you to see that our discovery is, at the very least, closely linked to the fact that there is no such thing as a sexual relationship, such as I defined it. Or, if you prefer, that the relationship between the sexes is speech itself. You can admit that this nevertheless leaves something to be desired. Moreover, I think you know quite a bit about it.

I have already established the fact that there is no relationship between the sexes by saying that there is currently no way in which to write such a relationship. There are people who dream that we will be able to write it someday. Who knows? Why not? Progress is occurring in biology – François Jacob is working at it, for example, isn't he? Perhaps someday there will no longer be any question regarding the sperm and the ovum. They are made for each other – it will be "written," as they say. That's what I ended with last time. Then you'll be happy, won't you? We can write science-fiction can't we? Try it. It's difficult to write, but why not? That's how people make headway.

Whatever the case may be, it can't be written currently without bringing in something a bit odd, because we don't know anything about its sex – namely, what is known as the phallus.

I would like to thank the person who pointed out the page number on which man's desire is written $\Phi(a)$ in my *Écrits* [p. 572]. Φ is the signifier "phallus." I'm saying this for those who believe that the phallus is the lack of a signifier [see Chapter II of this Seminar]. I know that this is debated in cartels. And woman's desire is written $A(\varphi)$ on the same page. (φ) is the phallus where we imagine it is, the little peepee. That's the most we can manage to write after, good Lord, something that I will simply call the fact of having arrived at a certain moment in science.

This moment is characterized by a certain number of written coordinates, at the top of the list being the formula Newton wrote concerning the gravitational field, which is nothing but a pure writing. No one has yet managed to provide any sort of substantial prop or the slightest shred of verisimilitude to what that writing enunciates, which seems up until now to be a bit tough, because no one can manage to envelope it in the schema of other fields in which people have more substantive ideas. The electromagnetic field provides us with images, doesn't it? Magnetism is always a bit animal. But the gravitational field isn't. It's quite curious. When I think that those guys, and soon those guys and gals, who are walking on that absolutely sublime place, the moon – which is certainly one of the incarnations of the sexual object – when I think that they go there carried by mere writing, that leaves room for a great deal of hope. Even in the field in which it could serve us – namely, desire. Anyway, it won't happen right away, will it? Despite psychoanalysis, it won't happen right away.

That is thus writing insofar as it is something we can talk about.

85

3

There is something that astonishes me, even though it is included in an incredible book.

It is the series of papers from an umpteenth Congrès de Synthèse [Thematic Congress], which is entitled quite simply *L'Écriture* ["Writing"]. It was published in Paris by Armand Colin in 1963 and is quite easy to get ahold of.

The first paper is by the dear, late Alfred Métraux, who was a fine and truly astute guy. In it, he talks a great deal about the writing of Easter Island. It's lovely.

He begins with the fact that he himself understands nothing about it, but that a few others have been a bit more successful; yet, naturally, their conclusions are debatable. But the fact that his apparently unsuccessful efforts are what actually authorize him to speak about what others have been able to draw out of it with debatable success constitutes an altogether marvelous example of the kind of modesty we should evince. Following his introduction, innumerable papers talk about each of the forms of writing. And, by Jove, it's all rather sensible.

People weren't immediately able to say rather sensible things about writing, and we shall see why. It surely required, in the interim, serious effects of intimidation, the kind that result from the incredible adventure we call science. There is not a single one of us in this room, me included, of course, who can have the slightest idea what will come of it.

Fine. Well, let's move on. People are going to protest a little about pollution, the future, a certain number of idiocies like that, and science will play a few practical jokes, regarding which it would not be altogether useless to see, for example, what science's relationship with writing is. It could serve some purpose.

Be that as it may, reading this thick collection of papers on writing, which is already at least ten years old, is truly a breath of fresh air compared with what is produced in linguistics. It is truly refreshing. It is not absolute trash. It is even very salubrious. After reading it, you truly cannot believe that writing isn't tantamount to representations of words. That seems like nothing, but since it is written everywhere and no one reads it, it is nevertheless worth saying. 86

The term *Wortvorstellung* should mean something to you. Freud employed it, saying that it is the secondary process. Naturally, everyone laughs, it being clear that Freud does not agree with Lacan. It is unfortunate, nevertheless, that, perhaps, in the circulation of your thoughts . . . You of course have thoughts. Some of you, those who have been around for quite a while, even have some knowledge. So you imagine that you represent words to yourselves [*vous vous représenter des mots*]. That's hysterically funny. Let's be serious. Writing is the representation of words.

It seems that no one has spelled out the consequences of this incredibly simple idea, consequences that are, nevertheless, quite visible. Let us consider all the languages that use something that we can take to be figures, and that are called, I don't remember what – pictograms or ideograms.

It is incredible, and has led to absolutely crazy consequences, that there are people who imagined that with logic – in other words, with the manipulation of writing – we would find a means by which to have what? "New ideas."* As if we didn't already have enough ideas!

When we study a bit of writing (a pictogram, ideogram, or whatever) we always find – and there are no exceptions – that it is pronounced as it is because it seems to depict something:

wu

Owing to the fact that it seems to depict your mother with two nipples, it is pronounced *wu*. After that, you do whatever you like with it. What difference does it make whether everything that is pronounced *wu* has two nipples and depicts your mother?

There is a guy – I think his name is Xu Shen, and this goes back a long way, all the way back to the beginning of the Christian era – who wrote something called *Shuo-wen*, in other words, "What is said qua writing." For *wen* is writing, isn't it?

87

wen

Try to copy it all the same, because, to the Chinese, knowing how to write is a sign of civilization. And they are right. Thus "word representation" means something: it means that the word is already there *before* you provide it with a written representation, with everything the latter brings with it. What it brings with it is what the author of *Shuo-wen* had already discovered at the beginning of our era. It is one of the most essential mainsprings of writing. The dear man still had his biases, for he imagined that there are written signs that resemble the things that the words designate.

For example, and I'll need some room to write this:

ren

What is it?

[A few people in the room reply.]

A man. They know a lot about it. People already taught them things. It's obvious, it's a man to you. What is represented here? What makes it an image of a man? We have here the head and then the legs. Okay. Why not? Some people are quite imaginative. Personally I see something more like a crotch there. Why not?

There is something funny, which is that we've had these signs since the Yin dynasty. We've had them a long time. Two thousand years have gone by, but they go back further, don't they? And we have still more of these signs. Which proves that they actually knew a great deal about writing. We can find these characters on tortoise shells. There were seers – people like us – who scrawled them next to other things found on tortoise shells to comment on them in writing. This probably gave rise to more effects than we think.

88   No matter. But there is something that, in fact, vaguely resembles something, for example, a man. I'm not sure why I am telling you this. I'm letting myself go, even though I have other things to tell you. Well, too bad; it's already done.

So there is something that you see there that might be able to pass itself off as a man. Cute, isn't it? Well, we follow his lead because, as you know, writing doesn't disappear from one day to the next. If you count on the audiovisual realm, you might end up with nothing.

You'll be dealing with writing for quite a while to come because, as I am telling you, it is the medium of science. Science is not going to leave its medium behind just like that. Our fate is going to be played out in the little doodles, as in the times of the Yin, the little scribblings that guys did in their corners, guys like me. There were plenty of them.

We are proceeding era by era. We trace things back to Zhou, and after him, we have the Qin, the era when people burned books. Qin was some guy! He got people to burn books. He had understood things; he was an emperor. He didn't last twenty years, and then writing immediately reappeared, and in an even more refined form. I won't go into all the different forms of Chinese writing. The close connection between writing and what people wrote with, reeds, is absolutely superb. Well, I don't want to get ahead of myself regarding the value of the reed as an instrument.

So we keep tracing things, and in the end, what do we find? We certainly don't find the guy that you were expecting, the cute little guy known as *ren*.

I may pronounce it well or badly; in any case, I didn't use the proper tone; my apologies if there is a Chinese person here. They are very sensitive to tone; it is even one of the ways of proving the primacy of speech. There are currently four different typical ways – typical, which doesn't mean that there aren't more in the Chinese world, and the fact that there are four suits me perfectly – to say *i*. *I* means four different things at once, which are not at all unrelated to each other. Well, I won't let myself fly off on that tangent.

Perhaps I will, for I'll refer to them once I've practiced the four pronunciations. [Lacan tries out the different pronunciations.]

There you have it. They don't all mean the same thing, but a very cultured man tells me that they play an important role in linguistic consciousness. Tone itself – and that is why we have to examine it 89 carefully before talking about arbitrariness – has a substantial indicative value to the Chinese. Why should we shy away from it when English, a language that is much closer to ours, presents modulatory effects that are quite seductive?

Naturally, it would be going too far to say that tone is related to meaning. For that to be true, we would have to grant the word "meaning" a weight that it doesn't have, since the miracle or marvel that proves that there is something to be done with language – namely, puns – relies on nonmeaning. If people took a look at a few other writings that were "rubblished" [*poubelliqués*, a combination of *poubelle* (garbage can or rubbish bin) and *published*], they might perhaps have concluded that it was no accident that I wrote "The Instance of the Letter in the Unconscious." I didn't entitle it "The

Instance of the Signifier," that dear signifier, that "Lacanian signifier," as people put it – as they put it when they want to claim that I
unjustifiably stole it from Saussure.

Right. The fact that a dream is a rebus, as Freud tells us, won't
stop me for a minute from saying that the unconscious is structured
like a language. But note that it is a language in the midst of which
its writing appeared. That does not, of course, mean that we should
have the slightest faith – and when would we? – in the figures that
parade around in our dreams. Once we realize that they are word
representations, they can be translated, *überträgt* – since they
constitute a rebus – into what Freud calls thoughts, *die Gedanken*,
unconscious thoughts.

What does it mean when you repeat a slip of the tongue, a
bungled action, or a slip-up in the psychopathology of everyday
life three times in five minutes? I don't know why I'm telling you
this, because it is an example that reveals something about one of
my patients. Not long ago, one of my patients called his mother
"my wife" for five minutes straight. Every time he did so, he cor-
rected himself and laughed, but it didn't matter to him. "She's not
my wife, because my wife," etc. and he went on like that for five
minutes. He must've made the same slip twenty times. In what way
can we say that such speech is bungled? I knock myself out telling
you that *that* is truly successful speech. Why? Because his mother
truly was his wife. He called her exactly what he ought to have
called her.

Something is bungled only in relation to what? In relation to the
speech prefigured by the astute people of "arche-writing," writing
that has always been out there in the world. It's a funny exercise,
isn't it? It's okay with me: it's one of the functions of academic dis
course to cloud the issue like that. Everybody fulfills his function. I
fulfill mine as well, and it, too, has its effects.

Fine. So we have a new figure of progress, which is the advent or
emergence in the world of a substitute for the idea of evolution that
locates us at the top of the animal totem pole, owing to our characteristic consciousness, thanks to which we shine with our proverbial
brilliance. It is the appearance in the world of programming.

I will comment that there can be no programming without writing
only in order to point out that, on the other hand, symptoms, slips,
bungled actions, and the psychopathology of everyday life have no
meaning or prop unless you begin with the idea that what you have
to say is programmed – in other words, has to be written. Of course,
if my patient wrote "my wife" instead of "my mother," he would
indubitably have made a slip, but there is no slip that is not a *lapsus
calami* [slip of the pen], even when it is a *lapsus linguae* [slip of the

tongue], because the tongue knows very well what it has to do. It is a little phallus that gently tickles. When it has to say something, it says it. A guy by the name of Aesop already said that it was the best and the worst [in "The Tongues"]. That means quite a few different things.

Whatever the case may be, you will believe me if you like, given my state of fatigue (which you have undoubtedly noticed), after having read from cover to cover all that stuff about writing – because I do that, don't I? I feel obliged to do so. (The only thing I've never talked about is the superego.) I feel obliged to read the whole thing. That's the way I am. I do so to be sure, sure of things that my everyday life experience teaches me and demonstrates, for I nevertheless have respect for scholars. One of them might have come up with something that runs counter – why not? – to an experience that is as limited, narrow, and short as the experience we have in our analytic consulting rooms.

We perhaps truly need to read widely. But I must say I can't impose that on anyone else; it's not kindly viewed by most people.

There is another book, *Le Débat sur les écritures et les hiéroglyphs au XVIIe et au XVIIIe siècles* ["The Debate on Writing and Hieroglyphics in the 17th and 18th Centuries"]. I hope you will all run out and read it, but you may not be able to find it because I myself had to have it sent to me from a library. It was brought out by the *École pratique des hautes études*, Section 6. S.E.V.P.E.N. is 91 stamped on the front cover, which must be their publishing arm, located at 13 rue du Four in Paris, assuming it exists. Well, you should, all the same, take the trouble now and then to read something, and you might as well read this 1965 book by Madeline V.-David. Enough said.

Owing to the fact that writing represents speech – which, as you can clearly see, I didn't stress – it is something that turns out not to be mere representation. "Representation" also signifies "repercussion," because it is not at all clear that, without writing, there would be words. It is perhaps representation that in and of itself constitutes words.

When you have familiarized yourself a bit with a language like the one I am currently learning (and I'm not absolutely sure that I am doing so because of my superego), Japanese, you see how writing can impact a spoken language, as it is constituted – this melodious language, which is a marvel of subtlety and ingenuity. When I think that it's a language in which adjectives are conjugated, and that I waited all these years to study it, I really don't know what I have done with my time up until now! I could never have hoped for anything more than adjectives that are conjugated. It's a language in which the inflections have something absolutely marvelous about them, which is that they parade around all by themselves.

What is known as the moneme [or: morpheme], there in the middle, can be changed. Give it a Chinese pronunciation, which is altogether different from the Japanese pronunciation, such that when you have before you a Chinese character, you pronounce it *onyomi* ["sound reading" (i.e., Chinese-derived reading)], or *kunyomi* ["learn reading" (i.e., native Japanese reading)] depending on the cases, which are always very precise. But for someone who comes along like me, there is no way to know which of the two to pick. You have to be initiated, but naturally only natives know.

Moreover, there can be two different Chinese characters. If you pronounce them *kunyomi* – in other words, as in Japanese – you absolutely cannot say to which of these Chinese characters the first syllable of what you said belongs, and to which the last syllable belongs; the one in the middle still less. It is the set of the two Chinese characters that dictates the Japanese pronunciation of a multisyllabic word, which we hear perfectly, it being a pronunciation that corresponds to two characters at the same time. For, owing to the idea that a Chinese character corresponds in theory to a sylla-
92 ble when you pronounce it as in Chinese, *onyomi*, it is hard to see, if you read it as in Japanese, why you would believe you were obliged to decompose this representation of words into syllables.

Well, this teaches you a great deal about the fact that spoken Japanese has been nourished by its writing. It has been nourished by it in what sense? Linguistically, of course – in other words, in the sense in which linguistics impacts spoken language [*atteint la langue*], in other words, always through writing.

You should realize that if Saussure turned out to be relatively justified in characterizing signifiers as arbitrary, it is only insofar as he was talking about written depictions. How could he have used his little bar in his illustration of the sign – which I have sufficiently used and abused, with the thing below and the thing above [signifier and signified] – if there were no writing?

I am saying all of this to remind you that, when I say there's no such thing as a metalanguage, this is as clear as day. It is enough for me to provide you with a mathematical demonstration for you to see that I am obliged to talk about it, because it is something written. If I didn't talk about it, I would never get my point across.

If I talk about it, it is not metalanguage at all. It is what we call – and what mathematicians, when they outline a logical theory, themselves call – discourse, everyday discourse, ordinary discourse.

This is the function of speech, insofar as it is applied – not in an altogether unlimited, undisciplined way (which is what I earlier

called "to demonstrate"), of course – to language. Writing is what is
at issue; it is what we talk about.

There is no metalanguage in the sense that we only talk about
language on the basis of writing [or: with writing as our point of
departure, *à partir de l'écriture*].

4

So I'm telling you all that. I must admit that this does not tire me
out, if you will, but it tires me a bit nevertheless.

You can believe me if you like, but upon awakening this morning,
after having read Madeline David's book until one in the morning,
I said to myself that it truly is no accident that my *Écrits* begin with
"The Seminar on 'The Purloined Letter.'" The letter is taken up
there in a different sense than the one employed in "The Instance of
the Letter in the Unconscious"; in the former, it is taken up in the
epistolary sense.

I'm not very energetic, having gone to bed late, after midnight, 93
and Gloria can attest to the fact that I spent from eight o'clock to
nine-thirty rereading "The Seminar on 'The Purloined Letter.'" It's
rather worthwhile and a bit clever. I never reread my own work, but
when I do, you can't imagine how much I admire myself. I worked
pretty hard on it, of course; it's quite sophisticated and not badly
done. When I wrote it – I no longer recall when, the date is indicated
there somewhere – it was, as usual, for the scoundrels at Sainte-
Anne Hospital. In any case, I finalized it in a place that I indicate
at the end, for I am conscientious: San Casciano, near Florence in
Italy. That truly spoiled my vacation. Well, as you know, I have a
tendency to spoil my vacations.

Listen, it's getting late, and I think it might be better for me to
talk to you about it next time.

But then, perhaps, who knows, it might tempt you to read it if I
say more now. It might be better for me not to tell you right away
where to look. I will do so anyway, because some of you might not
notice otherwise.

The letter I talked about there, the letter the Queen receives – you
have perhaps read the tale in question by Edgar Allan Poe – is, it
must be said, a rather curious letter. We never find out what was
written in it. That is absolutely essential: we never find out what's
inside. And everything suggests that the Queen is the only one who
knows what, in the end, is inside. Moreover, in order to get the
police to look for it, you understand, she must realize that it can't
tip anyone off about anything. The only hitch is that it clearly has a

meaning. And as it was a certain Duke of something or other who sent it to her, should the King, her good lord and master, get his hands on it, he may say to himself (even if he doesn't understand its contents), "there's something fishy going on here." And God only knows what that might lead to. I miss the old stories about what such things gave rise to back in the day – leading a queen to the scaffold, for example.

Fine. As I cannot summarize everything I wrote about what Poe wrote in his story "The Purloined Letter" – which I translated approximately as *la lettre en souffrance* ["the letter awaiting delivery" (or "the unclaimed letter"); see *Écrits*, p. 21] – read it between now and next time from the middle of page 21 to the end. That may allow me to continue to justify for you what is converging in my discourse today.

94   You have perhaps vaguely heard of the impact of the letter's movements, of its changing of hands. The minister swiped it from the Queen, after which Dupin, Poe's genius, intervenes, he being the craftiest of the crafty, yet not as crafty as all that. But Poe himself is crafty as the narrator of the story.

Here, let me open up a parenthesis. I will raise a little question, but one which is of very general import. Is the narrator of the story the person who wrote it? Ask yourself the question when reading Proust, for example. You really have to, because if you don't, you're screwed – you believe that the story's narrator is an ordinary Joe who is a bit asthmatic and rather idiotic in his adventures. It's true! Yet, when you've read Proust for a while, you get the impression that it isn't idiotic at all. It's not about what Proust says about the narrator; it's about something else. Well, let's leave that aside.

From page 21 to some other page, you will see that I talk about the conveyance of the letter – of the way in which the minister took it from the Queen, and how Dupin picks up where the minister left off – and about what happens to Dupin when he is the holder [or: keeper, *détenteur*] of the letter. *Détenteur* is a funny word, isn't it? It might mean to have the possibility of *détente* [détente or triggering]. Regarding the letter that I talk about from this page to that page, you will see that I am the one who wrote it. Did I know what I was doing?

I won't tell you. What I was talking about there was the phallus. And, to go even further, I will say that no one has ever spoken about it better. That is why I am asking you to have a look at it – it will teach you something.

March 10, 1971

VI

ON A FUNCTION THAT MUST
NOT BE WRITTEN

To mathematicians
The king as a subject
On written myths
On the no-more-than-one
On the two logics

I don't know what "The Seminar on 'The Purloined Letter'" can still yield.

Can you hear me in the fourth row? Great. At least we can all breathe easy. That will allow for more productive relations. For example, I might, in one case, ask someone to leave. And if things got really bad, I myself could have a fit and leave. The other auditorium gave the impression that there is a sexual relationship because, as in the majority of cases, people believe such a thing exists when they are crammed in a sardine can [*boî-boîte*]. That will allow me to ask you to raise your hands.

Who among you followed my explicit suggestion and made the effort to read pages 21 to 30 of what are known as my *Écrits*? Go ahead, raise your hands. You are allowed to raise hands here. I see there aren't that many of you. Perhaps I will throw a fit after all. I could simply split, since I have to keep at least some of my wits about me if I'm going to inquire what relationship you might have sensed exists between those pages and what I said I talked about in them – namely, the phallus.

Who is in the mood to say something about it? (You see, I am being kind, I'm not calling on anyone.) Or even about the fact, why not, that there is hardly any way to perceive the phallus in them? Would someone be kind enough to say a few words about, not what these pages, but what the fact that I said last time that I believe they concern the phallus, inspired him to think?

You there, did you reread those pages?

You didn't reread them? Beat it.

96   Well, it's very annoying. I am certainly not going to read them to you. That would really be asking too much of me. I am a little bit shocked, all the same, not to be able to get a response from anyone, without having to tease someone.

It's very annoying. Honestly!

1

I speak quite precisely in those pages about the function of the phallus only insofar as it is articulated in a certain discourse.

I hadn't yet even begun to construct, at that time, the whole range of the tetrahedral combination, with four apexes, that I presented last year [i.e., the four discourses]. I note, nevertheless, that, already at that level of my construction, already at that time, I took aim, as it were – to be able to shoot is already a big deal – in such a way that it seems to me to be not off-target even now, at a later stage of my construction.

Naturally, I hope you didn't take me literally when I said that I admired myself last time – I let myself go like that at times, especially when I must pretend to take a little breather. What I admired was, rather, that the path I laid down – at a time when I was just beginning to plow a certain furrow, based on specific landmarks – didn't need to be clearly rejected now, didn't make me feel ashamed. I ended last year on the topic of shame, which is quite remarkable. It might even encourage me the tiniest little bit to continue.

Every signifier that can be fished, so to speak, out of it is quite striking, and that is precisely what is at issue. I came to fish in the "Seminar on "The Purloined Letter,'" which – since I placed it at the front of my *Écrits*, breaking with a chronological presentation – I think perhaps showed that I thought it was the best introduction to my writings.

This leads me to the remark I make about the famous man "who dares all things, those unbecoming as well as those becoming a man." If I insisted at the time on translating it literally as *"ce qui est indigne aussi bien que ce qui est digne d'un homme,"* it was

97   because the formulation must obviously be taken as a whole. *The unspeakable, shameful thing that is not said about a man is clearly the phallus there.* To translate the formulation by breaking it into two as Baudelaire did in his translation of the story, *"ce qui est indigne d'un homme, aussi bien que ce qui est digne de lui,"* is not fitting. Nor must one break up the other formulation I quote: "the robber's knowledge of the loser's knowledge of the robber" (*"la connaissance qu'a*

le voleur de la connaissance qu'a le volé de son voleur" [*Écrits*, p. 24]).
Knowing that (s)he knows – in other words, knowing that one has
established a certain fantasy of oneself, that one is a man who dares
all things – is an element that is key to the situation, as Dupin says
immediately thereafter.

I said that, and I am not going to go back over it. For, in truth,
what I indicated there could have allowed people – people who
made an effort to study a text like that – to directly propose most
of the extensions that I will perhaps develop, unfold, and construct
today, as you will see later on. Once you have heard what I will
more or less have succeeded in saying, you will see that it was, in
short, already written there – and not simply written there, but supplied with all the necessary nexuses – indeed, the same ones through
which I believe I must guide you. Thus everything that is there is
not merely sifted and bound [*lié*], but well constructed with signifiers available for a more elaborate signification: the signification,
in short, of a teaching, my teaching, that I can qualify as having no
precedent, no other precedent than Freud's – precisely insofar as
Freud defines the preceding time [*la fois précédente*] in such a way
that we must read its structure in its impossibilities.

Can we, for example, say that Freud formulated the impossibility
of a relationship between the sexes, strictly speaking? No, he does
not formulate it as such. If I do so, it's simply because it's quite
simple to read, being written throughout his work. It is written in
what Freud wrote. All you have to do is read it. You will see later
why *you* don't read it. I will try to explain that and to explain why
I read it.

This little text begins with a letter that is "purloined" – not *volée*
[stolen], for, as I explain right at the outset, "purloined" means
"which is going to take a detour," or as I translate it, *la lettre "en
souffrance"* [the letter "awaiting delivery" (or the "unclaimed"
letter); *Écrits*, p. 21] – and ends with it nevertheless arriving at its
destination. I hope that a few more of you will read it between now
and the next time we meet, which will be a ways off because you
won't see me again until the month of May. You will have time to
read all forty pages of "The Purloined Letter."

At the end of my "Seminar on 'The Purloined Letter,'" I strive to 98
highlight what is essential in the story, and indicate why the French
translation of the title, *La Lettre volée*, is inadequate. "Purloined"
implies that the letter nevertheless arrives at its destination. And I
indicate what that destination is. It is the fundamental destination
of any and every letter – of the *epistolary* kind, that is. It lands, let
us say, in the hands of (not even he or she, but rather) those who
can understand nothing about it, including the police in this case.

Naturally, the police are totally unable to understand anything whatsoever about the substrate or matter of the letter. I highlight this and explain it in the course of numerous pages; this was precisely why the police were incapable of finding it. Poe's invention or forgery is magnificently described. The letter is, of course, beyond the scope of the explication of space, since that is what is at issue. That is what the police say initially, and this is then repeated by the Prefect. They are sure the letter must be at the minister's house, so that he will always have it within arm's reach. And they have literally divided up the space there into little numbered "compartments," without the letter being found.

It's funny, isn't it? Whenever I let myself fly off on a tangent, I end up commenting on space. And why not, after all?

Space has, since Descartes' time, been the most cumbersome thing in all creation for our logic. This is a fine time to talk about it – even if it must be added as a sort of marginal note – as what I dub the dimension of the imaginary.

There are people who are bothered, not necessarily by that particular paper of mine, but by others, or even by notes they have kept about what I said a while back about identification [in Seminar IX], for example. I must say that in 1961–1962, everyone in my audience was thinking about something else – except maybe one or two people who came from altogether different backgrounds and didn't know exactly what was going on. I spoke back then about the "unary trait." And it seems that people are now bothered, quite legitimately, about where this unary trait should be situated, in the symbolic or the imaginary? And why not the real? Whatever the case may be, it's like a stick [*bâton* (Lacan presumably draws a single horizontal or vertical line on the board)], since this is what *ein einziger Zug* looks like. I fished it out of Freud's work, naturally.

This raises several questions, as I began to say last time, commenting that it was altogether impossible to tenably maintain a bipartition between logic and mathematics, which is so difficult and problematic for mathematicians. Is everything reducible to pure logic – in other words, to a discourse that is propped up by a clearly determined structure? Isn't there an absolutely essential element that remains, no matter what we do to include it in the structure and eliminate it? Isn't there a central core that remains, all the same, which is known as intuition?

This is assuredly the question that Descartes took as his point of departure. I would point out that, in his view, mathematical reasoning derived nothing effective, creative, or in any way relevant to reasoning, but solely it's the point of departure – namely, an original intuition, the one he posited and established – from his initial distinction between space [or: extension, *l'étendue*] and thought. This Cartesian opposition, forged more by a thinker than by a mathematician – although he was certainly not unproductive in the field of mathematics, as the facts have shown – has, naturally, been greatly filled out by mathematicians themselves. It was truly the first time that philosophy contributed something to mathematics. I beg you to note something that seems very clear to me – please correct me if you can, for it would be easy to find people who are far more competent in this area than I am – which is that mathematicians in Antiquity made headway in their field without concerning themselves in the slightest with what was happening in any of the schools of wisdom or philosophy. This is not the case in our times, for Descartes' distinction between intuiting and reasoning has assuredly had a strong influence on mathematics itself.

This is why I cannot fail to find a furrow therein, which is the effect of something that has a certain relationship with what I attempt to do here in our field. It seems to me that the remark I can make – from where I stand regarding the relations between speech and writing, concerning, at least, along this first ridge [*arête*], what is unusual in the function of writing with regard to all discourse – is perhaps of such a nature as to get mathematicians to realize what I indicated last time, which is that the very intuition of Euclidean space owes something to writing.

Moreover, what is known in mathematics as the logical simplification [*réduction*] of mathematical operations has no other prop than the manipulation of lowercase and uppercase letters from varied alphabets – I mean Greek letters or Germanic letters, indeed several alphabets. You can observe this by familiarizing yourself with its history. Every manipulation by which logic simplifies things in mathematical reasoning requires this prop. I'm going to try to take this a bit further for you.

As I have repeatedly said, I see no essential difference between that and what – for a long time, for a whole era, the seventeenth and eighteenth centuries – posed a problem for mathematical thought: the need for drawings in Euclidean demonstrations. At least one triangle had to be drawn. People would get up in arms about this. Was the triangle that was drawn a general triangle or a particular triangle? It is quite clear that it is always particular. What you demonstrate regarding triangles in general is always the same story: their three angles are equivalent to two right angles. Yet it is clear that you must not say that a specific triangle has no right to simultaneously be an orthogonal isosceles triangle or an equilateral triangle. Thus it is always particular.

This bothered mathematicians enormously. I won't dwell on it here, naturally. This is not the place to recall it to mind, for we are not here to engage in erudite discussions of all those who weighed in on this after Descartes: Leibniz and others, and later Husserl. It nevertheless seems to me that they never noticed a hitch: writing is there on both sides, homogenizing intuiting and reasoning. In other words, writing little letters has no less intuitive a function than the figures that dear old Euclid drew. We must nevertheless figure out why people think that makes a difference.

I don't know if I should point out that the consistency of space – of Euclidean space, of space that is limited to three dimensions – seems to me to have to be defined in an entirely different way. If you take two points, they are equidistant from each other, so to speak: the distance from the first to the second is the same as the distance from the second to the first. You can take three points and situate them in such a way that that is still true – namely, that each point is equidistant from the two others. You can do the same with four in such a way that it is still true. (I've never heard anyone explicitly say that.) You can take five, but don't rush here to say that you can also situate them equidistantly from each other because you can't, at least not in our Euclidean space. To have five points equidistant from each other, you have to fabricate a fourth dimension. There you have it.

Naturally, it is quite easy to literally fabricate one, and it holds up quite nicely. We can demonstrate that a space with four dimensions is perfectly coherent, in the sense that we can demonstrate a link between its coherence and the coherence of real numbers. This is precisely why it holds up.

What is obvious is that, beyond a tetrahedron, intuition already needs to be propped up by letters.

2

I started out in this direction because I said that the letter that arrives at its destination is the letter that lands in the hands of the police who don't understand anything about it.

The police have, as you know, been around for a long time. If you've read a little bit of what Hegel wrote, you realize that three pikes [or: spears] on the ground, or three pikes on campus, are tantamount to the State. To anyone who has given it the slightest bit of thought – and we cannot accuse Hegel of being a slacker in that regard – the State and the police are one and the same thing. This is based on a tetrahedral structure [the master's discourse].

Stated otherwise, as soon as we call something like the letter into question, we must trot out my little schemas from last year, which were designed, as you recall, as follows:

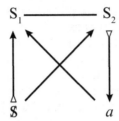

Figure 6.1 The Master's Discourse

This is the master's discourse, as you perhaps remember. It is characterized by the fact that one of the six edges [arêtes] of the tetrahedron is broken [the one connecting $ and a]. It is to the degree to which we make these structures rotate along [one of] the four edges of the circuit that are continuous in the tetrahedron – this is a condition – and turn in the same direction, that variation in the structure of discourse is established, precisely insofar as it remains at a certain level of construction, which is the tetrahedral level. We cannot confine ourselves to this level once we bring out the instance of the letter. It is even because we cannot confine ourselves to this level that, if we do, there is always one of the segments of what constitutes a circle that is broken [the "circle" constituted by the four mathemes].

It is on that basis that we see that, in a world structured by a certain tetrahedron, the letter arrives at its destination only by finding the person who, in my paper on "The Purloined Letter," I designated with the term "subject." He must not be eliminated or withdrawn in any way, with the excuse that we are making a few steps forward in the structure. If what we have discovered that goes by the name of the unconscious has a meaning, we cannot, even at this level, fail to take into account the subject who is, let me repeat, ineliminable. But the subject is distinguished by his highly specific imbecility. That is what counts in Poe's text, owing to the fact that the person poked fun at on this occasion is the King – and this is no accident – who appears here as a subject [p. 28].

He understands absolutely nothing, and the whole of his police force is unable to make it such that the letter falls into his hands, given that it is the police who are holding it and can do nothing with it. I would go so far as to highlight that even if it were to be found in the police's files, it could not serve any purpose to the historian [p. 28]. On one page or another of what I wrote about that letter, I mentioned that it is quite probable that the Queen is the only one who knows what it means [p. 29]. What gives it its importance is that were the only person that it concerns – namely, the subject, the King – to have it in hand, he would understand solely that it surely has a meaning, a meaning that escapes him as a subject (this is what is scandalous therein). The terms "scandal" and "contradiction" are in their proper place [p. 23] in the last four short pages – I am emphasizing their brevity – that I asked you to read.

Since a few of you here read Poe in the past, you must recall that there is a Minister involved, the one who swiped the letter. It is clear that it is owing solely to the circulation of the letter that the Minister evinces, in the course of the movements of that letter, variations, like the variations in color of a moving fish. In truth, its essential function, which my text plays on a bit excessively – but one can never overly stress something if one is to convey one's point – revolves around the fact that the letter has a feminizing effect.

Yet as soon as he no longer has the letter (without knowing it), we see him restored, in some sense, to the dimension that his whole scheme was designed to give him, that of "the man who dares all things." Let me emphasize the shift in what occurs, for this is where Poe's story ends. It is at that moment that the thing appears, the *monstrum horrendum*, as it says in the text.

This is what he wanted to be for the Queen, who, of course, took note of this, since she tried to get the letter back. But he kept the game going. So it was up to Dupin – namely, the slyest of the sly, the one to whom Poe grants the role of doing something that I will willingly call, as I do in the text, "hoodwinking" us [p. 11]. Namely, that we believe that the slyest of the sly exists, that he truly understands and knows everything, that, even while he is in the tetrahedron, he can understand how it is constructed.

I made enough ironic remarks about Poe's very adept play on words with *ambitus, religio,* and *honesti homines* [p. 14] to simply say that I myself was looking for the rub [*la petite bête*] somewhere else, wasn't I? In truth, it is somewhere. It is somewhere if we follow Poe, and we can wonder whether Poe himself realized this.

Namely, that, owing to the simple fact of having passed into Dupin's hands, the letter feminized him, in turn. And it did this so thoroughly that it was precisely at that moment that he could no longer contain himself and manifested some rage at the Minister [p. 29] – a man who believed he already had everyone at his mercy, such that he had no need to leave any further trace – even though Dupin knew he had deprived the Minister of what would have allowed him to continue to play his role if he'd ever had to show his cards. He sent him a message [a quote from Crébillon's play *Atrée*] in the letter that he substituted for the letter he swiped:

Un dessein si funeste
S'il n'est digne d'Atrée, est digne de Thyeste.

So fatal a scheme,
If not worthy of Atreus, is worthy of Thyestes.

The question, as it were, is whether Poe clearly realizes here the import of the fact that Dupin sends a sort of message beyond all possibilities, for God only knows if the Minister will ever take out Dupin's letter and suddenly find himself deflated [p. 27]. Which tells you that castration is, like the letter, in abeyance [*suspendue*] here, even though it is perfectly well realized.

I would also indicate that this doesn't seem to me to be deter- 104 mined in advance. Which merely makes all the more significant what Dupin writes by way of a message to the person who he has just deprived of what he believes to be his power. This little gumshoe [or: private eye, *petit poulet*] is thrilled at the idea of what will happen when the Minister will have to use it – before whom and with what aim? What we can say is that Dupin is enjoying himself [*jouit*]. Here arises once again the question I broached last time when I asked whether the narrator and the author are one and the same. What is indisputable here is that the narrator – the subject of the statement, the one who is speaking – is Poe. Does Poe get off on Dupin's jouissance, or on something else? That is what I'm going to strive to show you today.

I am talking to you about "The Purloined Letter" as I myself laid it out for you. This illustrates the question I raised last time. Aren't the author and he who speaks in his name as the narrator in a written text radically different? Their difference is palpable here.

Indeed, what occurs at the level of the narrator is, in the final analysis, what I might call – excuse me for emphasizing the demonstrative character of this little essay – the most perfect castration. That is demonstrated here. Everyone is equally deceived, unbeknownst to them [p. 11].

It is clear that the King has been asleep since the beginning, naturally, and will continue to sleep like a log till the end of his days.

The Queen does not realize that she is pretty much doomed to fall head over heels for the Minister, now that she has him in her power, now that she has castrated him. He's a dear [*c'est un amour*].

The Minister's goose is cooked, but he couldn't care less, in the end, because, as I explain very clearly somewhere, only one of the two following things can be the case: either he will be happy to become the Queen's lover, which should be pleasant (in theory, anyway; people say that, yet, naturally, it doesn't please everyone); or, if he feels for her one of the feelings that I consider to be the only lucid ones – namely, hatred, as I have very plainly explained [p. 30] – if he hates her, she will love him all the more for it. Which will allow him to go so far that he will end up suspecting, nevertheless, that the letter has no longer been in his possession for quite a while. For he will be mistaken, naturally. He will tell himself that, if she has gone this far with him, she must be sure of things, and then he will open his little piece of paper in time. But in no case will he do what Dupin wants him to do: make a fool of himself [p. 11]. He will not make himself look ridiculous.

Fine. That is what I have managed to say about what I wrote. And what I would like to say to you now is that it takes on its import because it is illegible [or: unreadable, *illisible*].

That is the point that I will now try to lay out, if you are still willing to listen.

3

I will go straight to the point. Distinguished people [*Les gens du monde*] are the only ones who are able to tell me what they think about what I palm off on them.

When my *Écrits* had not yet come out, they gave me their opinion as practitioners. "We don't understand a word of it," they told me.

That's significant. Something about which we understand nothing leaves room for hope – it is the sign that we are affected by it. We are fortunate not to understand anything, because we can only understand what we already have in our heads. Still, I would like to articulate this a bit better.

It is not enough to deliberately write something incomprehensible. We have to see why what is illegible has a meaning. Let me point out, first of all, that our whole business, centered as it is on the relationship between the sexes, revolves around the fact that you might believe that it is written.

That is, in short, what people found in psychoanalysis. They located a written text. *Totem and Taboo* is a written myth. And I would go even further: that is the only thing that specifies it. We might have taken up any old myth, as long as it was written. The characteristic of a myth that is written, as Claude Lévi-Strauss has pointed out, is that when you write it, there is only one version of it; whereas the characteristic of myths – as all of Lévi-Strauss's work strives to demonstrate – is that there is a large quantity of spoken versions of them. That is what constitutes *Totem and Taboo* as a written myth.

This written myth could very well pass itself off as the inscription of the relationship between the sexes [*rapport sexuel*]. But I would, nevertheless, like to point out certain things.

If it was no accident that I took the text of "The Purloined Letter" 106 as my point of departure, it was because – since the letter can, in this case, take on a feminizing function – *Totem and Taboo*, qua written myth, is designed very precisely to indicate that it is unthinkable to say Woman [La *femme*].

Why is it unthinkable? Because one cannot say "all women." One cannot say "all women" because this appears in the myth only insofar as the Father possesses "all the women," which is the clear sign of an impossibility.

On the other hand, what I underscore regarding "The Purloined Letter" is that, if there is only *a* woman and not Woman – in other words, if the function of woman can only be deployed on the basis of what the great mathematician Luitzen Egbertus Jan Brouwer, in the context of what I said earlier about mathematical discussion, calls the "multi-unit," there is a function that is, strictly speaking, that of the Father, who is there. The Father is there to get his radical function recognized, the function he has always manifested in the context of monotheism, for example.

It's no accident that Freud foundered here. It was because there is an altogether essential function that must be reserved as being, strictly speaking, at the origin of writing. It is what I will call the "no-more-than-one."

Aristotle, of course, strove to render that accessible to us by gradual steps, as he usually did. He did so in the name of a principle that we can call his principle of proceeding back (along the ladder) from one cause to another and from one being to the next, until we have to stop somewhere. He was very kind in that way. He was truly catering to imbeciles. Hence the development of the function of the subject.

The no-more-than-one arises right from the outset. Without the no-more-than-one, you can't even begin to write the series of whole numbers. I will show you that on the blackboard next time. There has to be a 1, and then you need but beat your head against the wall [literally, drop dead with your lips forming a circle, *crever la bouche en rond*] whenever you want to begin anew, so that every time it makes 1 more, but not the same 1. But all those that are repeated in this way are the same, and can be added together. We call that the arithmetic series.

107   But let us return to what seems to me to be essential on this topic, concerning sexual jouissance.

There is, experience tells us, but one structure, regardless of its specific presentation. Sexual jouissance turns out to be unwritable, which is what gives rise to structural multiplicity – the tetrad, first of all, in which something is sketched out that situates it, but which remains inseparable from a certain number of functions that have, in short, nothing to do with what can generally specify the sexual partner.

The structure is such that actual men, insofar as they function, are castrated; and on the other hand, something exists at the level of the female partner, and which can simply be drawn with this line on which I indicate the import of the whole function of the letter in this case: *La* femme [Woman] has nothing to do – assuming she exists, which is why she doesn't exist – with the law.

How, then, can we conceptualize what has happened? People make love all the same, don't they? People do make love and we realize what poses a problem as soon as we look into it. People have been looking into it for a long time, and they have perhaps always looked into it, except that we have lost the key to how they did it before. But for us, at the heart and flourishing of the scientific era, we perceive what it is through Freud. What forms an obstacle to the sexual relationship when we try to structure it and make it function by means of symbols? The fact that jouissance gets involved.

Can sexual jouissance be dealt with [or: treated, *traitée*] directly? No, and that's why – let us say, adding nothing further – there is speech. Discourse begins because there is a gap here. We can't remain at this point, I mean that I refuse to look to some sort of point of origin; but after all, nothing can stop us from saying that it is because discourse begins that the gap is produced. The result is the same. What is clear is that discourse is clearly connected to the gap, and since there is no such thing as a metalanguage, it cannot leave the gap behind.

What renders obvious what I am in the process of articulating about the symbolization of sexual jouissance is that it borrows all of its symbolism from what? From something that does not concern it – namely, from jouissance insofar as it is prohibited by certain

108   bewildering things. They are bewildering, but not that bewildering, for we have managed to articulate them perfectly well with the term "pleasure principle," which has but one meaning: not too much jouissance. Indeed, the very fabric of all jouissances borders on suffering; that is the very thing that allows us to recognize its trappings [*habit*]. If a plant does not plainly suffer, we cannot know it is alive.

It is thus clear that sexual jouissance can be structured only with reference to the prohibition, qua named, of jouissance, the prohibition of a jouissance that does not fall under the heading, strictly speaking, of lethal jouissance. Stated otherwise, sexual jouissance derives its structure only from the prohibition that concerns jouissance involving your own body – in other words, very precisely, at the limit [arête] or border where it verges on lethal jouissance. And it intersects the sexual dimension only by bringing prohibition to bear on the body from which your own body comes – namely, your mother's body. The only thing that can bring the law to bear there – namely, sexual jouissance – is structured and met up with anew in discourse by that alone.

In this case, your partner is effectively reduced to "one" [or: 1, une] – but not just any old which one: the one who gave birth to you. Everything that can be articulated is constructed around that, as soon as we enter into the field in a way that is verbalizable. Once we have made a bit more headway, I will return to the way in which knowledge comes to function as an enjoyment [un jouir]. We can skip that here.

Woman as such finds herself in the uniquely solid [or: compact (or amassed), rassemblée] position of being, I would say, subject to speech. I am sparing you the details. The fact that speech is what instates a dimension of truth – the impossibility of a relationship between the sexes – is also what makes for the import of speech, in the sense that it can do anything and everything except serve at the point that occasioned it. Speech strives to reduce women to subjection [or: subordination] – in other words, make them into something from which we expect signs of intelligence, if I may express myself thusly. But this naturally concerns no real being here.

To tell you exactly what I think, Woman in this case – as my text is designed to demonstrate, and I mean Woman as in-herself [en-soi], as if one could say "all women," Woman who does not (let me remind you) exist – is the letter, the letter insofar as it is the signifier that there is no Other, S(Ⱥ).

It is on that topic that, before leaving you today, I would like to 109 say something that traces out the logical configuration of what I am proposing.

4

In Aristotelian logic, you have the propositional categories. I am not writing them on the board with the letters that have become standard in formal logic. For example, I am not using A for the universal affirmative, but rather U.A. I am using U.N. for the universal negative – that's what that means. And I am using P.A. for particular affirmative and P.N. for particular negative. Let me point out that in Aristotle's discussion, it is between these two poles, U.A. and P.N., that things can be differentiated at the logical level.

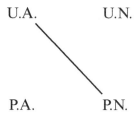

U.A.   U.N.

P.A.   P.N.

Figure 6.2 Aristotle's Logic of Propositions

The universal affirmative enunciates an essence. I have often emphasized in the past the nature of the statement "every line is vertical," mentioning the fact that it is perfectly compatible with the existence of no lines [see the upper two quadrants in Figure 4.2]. Essence is essentially situated in logic. It is a purely discursive statement.

The essential axis of logical differentiation in Aristotle's work is the oblique axis that I just drew on the board. Nothing runs counter to any identifiable logical statement if not the remark that "there are some that . . . aren't." This is the particular negative: "there are lines that are not vertical" [see the lower two quadrants in Figure 4.2]. It is the only way to contradict the assertion that it is an essential fact [i.e., to contradict the assertion that "every line is vertical"].

In the functioning of Aristotle's logic, the other two terms are altogether secondary. Namely "there are some that . . ."; that is a particular affirmative [see the two quadrants on the right in Figure 4.2], and how can we know if it is necessary or not? It doesn't prove anything. And the universal negative, "there are none that . . ." [see the two quadrants on the left in Figure 4.2]. Which is not the same as to say "there are some that . . . aren't" – it doesn't prove anything either, that's a fact.

What I can point out is what happens when we shift from Aristotelian logic to the transposition of propositions in mathematical logic, the kind that was constructed on the basis of what are known as "quantifiers." (Don't yell at me, because you won't be able to hear me anymore.) I am going to write them first, and writing is precisely what we are concerned with here.

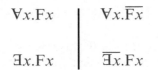

Figure 6.3 Logic of the Quantifiers

The universal affirmative is now going to be written with this unverbalizable notation, ∀. It's an upside down A. I say, "an upside down A," but it is not discourse, it is writing. It signals us, as you will see, to blather.

∀x.F(x) is the universal affirmative.

∃x.F(x) is the particular affirmative.

I want to express that ∀x.$\overline{F(x)}$ is a negative. How can I? I am struck by the fact that this has never been truly articulated as I am going to articulate it. You must place the bar of negation over the $\overline{F(x)}$ and not over both parts [i.e., not over both ∀x and F(x)], as is usually done. You will see why.

Lastly, it is over the ∃x that you have to place the bar of negation.

I myself am now placing a line [*barre*] equivalent to the one that was here [in Figure 6.2], separating the group of four into two zones [see Figure 6.3]. In this way, I am dividing them up by twos differently.

What I am stating is that in this way of writing, everything depends on what one can say regarding writing.

The distinction between the two terms that are united by the period in what is written ∀x.F(x) has the value of indicating that one can say about every x – this is signaled by the upside down A – that it satisfies what is written as F(x) and is not improper [*déplacé*].

The same is true for the particular, ∃x.F(x), but with a different accent. The accent of writing bears here on the fact that there is something that can be written – namely, that there exist x's that you can make function in F(x). You talk about them thus, in the quantifying transposition of Aristotelean logic, by means of quantifiers related to the particular. 111

Changing the way of dividing up the four terms hinges on writing. As for what is brought to the fore and considered acceptable, nothing changes regarding the universal. It is still valuable, even if it doesn't have the same value.

On the contrary, regarding what is at stake here, ∀x.$\overline{F(x)}$, the split consists in perceiving the nonvalue of the universal negative, since here, no matter what x you talk about, you must not write F(x).

The same is true for the particular negative. Just as here, in ∃x.F(x), the x could be written and was acceptable and inscribable in the formula, in $\overline{\exists x}.F(x)$ it is simply said that x cannot be written.

What does that mean? In both ways of laying this out, something remained in some sense overlooked and valueless, which is the universal negative insofar as it allows us to say that we must not write $F(x)$ if we talk about any x whatsoever. In other words, we have an essential cut [or: gap (or exclusion), *coupure*] here.

Well, that is the very thing around which the sexual relationship revolves.

We are interested here in what cannot be written in the function $F(x)$, when the function $F(x)$ itself must not be written. In this regard, it is what I stated earlier, which is the point we will return to when I see you in two months – namely, it is what is strictly speaking known as illegible.

March 17, 1971

VII

CLASS ON *"LITURATERRE"*

The word I just wrote on the board is the title of what I will present today, since, having asked you to convene here, I feel obliged to throw something your way.

My title was obviously inspired by things that are being talked about these days. It is the title with which I strove to satisfy a request made of me to write the introduction to an upcoming issue of the journal *Littérature* on the topic of literature and psychoanalysis.

Lituraterre is a word I invented, and it is justified by Alfred Ernout and Antoine J. Meillet's etymological dictionary of Latin. Some of you here may have heard of it. Look up the words *lino*, *litura*, and then *liturarius* in it. You will see clearly indicated there that none of them have anything to do with *littera*, letter. I couldn't care less whether they do or they don't. I don't necessarily bow to etymology when I allow myself to make the kinds of plays on words that lead at times to witticisms – like the obvious spoonerism [*contrepet*], *m'en revenant aux lèvres et le renversement à l'oreille* [literally: returning to my lips and inverting in my ears].

It's no accident that when you learn a foreign language, you sometimes inadvertently put the first sound of something you heard second, and the second first ["literature" becomes "lituraterre" by switching the *e* and the *u*].

Take a look at that dictionary, for it offers me auspices, being founded, as it is, on the same point of departure [*départ*] as my initial one. Take "departure" here in the sense of distributed [or: left behind (or divided up), *réparti*] – departing on the basis of an equivocation by which James Joyce slips from "a letter"* to "a litter,"* from letter to garbage.

There was – as you perhaps recall, but it's more likely you never knew anything about it – a benefactor who was well intentioned toward Joyce and offered to pay for his analysis, with Carl Jung to boot. Joyce would have gained nothing from the wordplay I

mentioned, because he went directly – with his "a letter, a litter"* –
to what we can expect at the end of an analysis, in the best of cases.

In turning the letter into litter [or: making litter (or bedding) of
the letter (or sacrificing the letter, or multiplying the letter), *À faire
litière de la lettre*], was Joyce once again thinking of Saint Thomas
Aquinas – as you may remember, if you ever knew it, *sicut palea*,
like chaff or manure – as his work attests he often did? Or was it,
114 instead, psychoanalysis, attesting to its convergence with what our
era evinces by way of a weakening of the ancient bond by which pollution was contained in culture?

I riffed on that, as if coincidentally, shortly before May 1968, in
order not to leave in the lurch the clueless crowd that flocked to see
me that day, as happens whenever I give a talk somewhere now. In
that instance, it was in Bordeaux. I reminded my audience right at
the outset that civilization begins with the sewer.

I should undoubtedly mention that this was shortly after my
October 1967 proposal ["Proposition du 9 octobre 1967 sur le
psychanalyste de l'École" in *Autres Écrits* (Paris: Seuil, 2001)] had
been received in the way you've heard about. This is tantamount to
telling you that, by riffing on that, I was a bit weary of the dumpster
to which I had tied my fate. Nevertheless, people know that I am not
the only one to admit [*l'avouer*] that it is my lot [*partage*], to admit
[*l'avouère*] – to pronounce it the way *avoir* used to be pronounced –
the plus column [or: credit, *l'avoir* (which is a homonym of *lavoir*,
washhouse or washtub)] that Beckett weighs in the scales against
the minus column [or: debit, *doit*] that makes our being into trash
[or: garbage, *déchet*]. This *avouère* allows literature to save face, and
it relieves me – which suits me just fine – of the privilege I might
believe I reap from my position.

We need to know whether the notion that textbooks, since they
first came into being (I'm talking about literature textbooks), have
promoted – namely, that literature is nothing but the reheating of
leftovers – stems from written collocations of what were, at the
outset, songs, spoken myths, and dramatic processions.

The fact that psychoanalysis hinges on Oedipus, the Oedipus
of the myth, in no way qualifies analysts to grasp Sophocles'
play. Psychoanalysis and literature are not the same. No one can
claim that literary criticism, which has heretofore been the exclu-
sive domain of university discourse, has received a new lease on
life from psychoanalysis just because Freud mentions a book by
Dostoyevsky.

Here, however, I am teaching in the midst of a sea change that
– colored by things that are being talked about these days – is currently being advertised as touting writing. But this change – which

is attested to, for example, by the fact that Rabelais is finally being read again now – shows that it is perhaps related to a literary shift that suits me better.

As an author, I am less involved in that sea change than people imagine, and my title, *Écrits*, is more ironic than people think, since the volume basically consists of papers given at conferences or (let's say that I would prefer they be understood as) "open letters" in each of which I present a portion of my teaching. That sets the tone, in any case.

Far be it from me, at any rate, to engage in the kind of literary forays made by psychoanalysts lacking in inventiveness. I decry their attempts, which never fail to demonstrate that their practice is not up to the task of inspiring [or: justifying, *motiver*] the slightest literary judgment.

It is nevertheless striking that I opened the collection of my papers entitled *Écrits* with an article that I took out of chronological order – whereas chronology reigns in the rest of the volume – and that revolves around a story which, it must be said, is quite peculiar, because it does not fit into the nice orderly list of dramatic situations – you are aware that such a list has been drawn up. Well, let's leave that aside.

The story is based on what happens when a letter is mailed to a specific individual, who is aware that it gets forwarded, and on terms that allow me to say, regarding this letter, that a letter always arrives at its destination, after detours that it undergoes in the tale [*conte*]. The account [*compte*, a homonym of *conte*], so to speak, is tallied without ever resorting to the letter's content. This is what makes it remarkable that the illusory effect the letter has on those who, one after the other, have it in their possession – the power that it confers impelling them to lay claim to it – can only be articulated, as I articulate it, as an effect of feminization.

Please excuse me for returning to this, but this requires us to distinguish – I am talking about what I do – the letter from the master signifier, insofar as the letter in this case bears the master signifier in its envelope, since what is at stake here is a letter in the epistolary sense. Now I submit that I do not make metaphorical use of the word "letter" in my text, because Poe's tale involves the fact that the message is conveyed as if by magic; only its written form – the letter, strictly speaking – makes unplanned stops [*fait seule péripétie*].

My criticism, if there be reasons to think it literary, thus cannot concern anything other – at least so I strive – than what Poe does, being a writer himself, in shaping such a message about the letter. It is clear that by not actually spelling it out the way I do, Poe states it – not insufficiently, but, rather, all the more rigorously.

Nevertheless, the elision, the elision of this message cannot be elucidated by means of any detail whatsoever of his psychobiography. This elision would, instead, be occluded thereby. You may recall that Marie Bonaparte, a psychoanalyst who scoured other texts by Poe, laid down her scouring pad here. The scullery maid didn't go near it.

116   So much for Poe's text.

Couldn't *my* text be explained by *my* psychobiography? My wish, for example, to be suitably read someday? But for that to be the case, he who would proffer such an interpretation would first have to explain what I contend the letter bears in order to always arrive, as I say, at its destination.

It is here that I perhaps agree, for the time being, with the sanctimonious writing squad. Psychoanalysis could learn an initial lesson from literature, which would, owing to repression, involve a less psychobiographical idea.

For my part, if I offer up Poe's text, along with what lies behind it, to analysts, it is precisely because psychoanalysis can only broach it by exposing its failure. This is how I shed light on psychoanalysis; people know that I know that I invoke the Enlightenment on the back jacket of my *Écrits*. Nevertheless, I shed light on psychoanalysis by demonstrating where it makes holes. There is nothing illegitimate about that. Holes have borne fruit – as we have known for a long time – in optics as well as in the most recent physics, that involving the photon.

Psychoanalysis could better justify its incursions into the field of literary criticism by adopting this method. Which would mean that literary criticism would, in fact, be renewed by psychoanalysis's existence, texts being measured against it, precisely insofar as the enigma remains on its side, staying silent.

But those analysts on whom I would not be casting aspersions by saying that, rather than practicing psychoanalysis, they receive practice from it [or: are trained (or worked over) by it, *en sont exercés*], fail to understand my work, at least on the whole.

To them, I propose an opposition between truth and knowledge. It is in the first that they immediately recognize their trade [or: employ, *office*], whereas I put their truth in the hot seat. In order to correct my aim, I would rather say "knowledge in check" [or: "knowledge at bay," *savoir en échec*], for that is where psychoanalysis shows itself to its best advantage. Knowledge in check, like people say *figure en abyme*, does not mean the failure of knowledge [*échec du savoir*]. I immediately hear that people conclude from the former that they have no need to evince any knowledge whatsoever.

Is it insignificant that I entitled one of the morsels I dubbed writings [*Écrits*], "the instance of the letter," as the unconscious's ratio [or: reason, *raison*]? Doesn't that sufficiently designate what, because it has to insist, is not fully within its rights to be in the letter, despite strong reasons for being so [or: regardless of how obvious this is, *si fort de raison que ça s'avance*]? To call that ratio mean or extreme [as in Euclid's *Elements*, Book VI, Definition 3] is to show, as I did at one time [in Seminar XIV], the bifid nature of any and all   117 measurement. But isn't there anything in reality [*réel*] that can do without this mediation?

A border, perhaps. A border, by separating two territories, has but one flaw, yet it is a sizable one. It symbolizes that the two territories are made of the same stuff, as it were, for whoever crosses the border, at any rate. I don't know if you've ever noticed this, but it is the principle that led a certain von Uexküll to coin the term *Umwelt* [outer world]. The *Umwelt* is designed to reflect the *Innenwelt* [inner world], and elevates borders to the rank of ideology. This is obviously an inauspicious point of departure: we have here a form of biology (for von Uexküll wished to found a form of biology on this basis) that takes all kinds of things for granted right from the outset – the fact of adaptation, in particular, that provides the foundation of this *Umwelt–Innenwelt* couple. Selection obviously is no better from an ideological standpoint. It is not because it generously dubs itself "natural" that it is any less ideological.

I am going to propose something quite brutally before coming to "a letter, a litter."

Isn't the letter the literal that must be based on the littoral? For it is something other than a border. You may, moreover, have noticed that we never confuse these things. The littoral is what posits the whole of one domain as constituting a border for another domain, if you will, but precisely because they have absolutely nothing in common, not even a mutual relationship.

Isn't the letter littoral, strictly speaking? Isn't that what the letter traces out – the edge of the hole in the kind of knowledge that psychoanalysis designates when it approaches it?

It is funny to note that psychoanalysis, in its very own movement, obliges itself, in some sense, to misrecognize the meaning of what the letter nevertheless says "to the letter" – that's the word for it – when all its interpretations boil down to jouissance. Between jouissance and knowledge, the letter would constitute [or: would (seem or like to) play the part of, *ferait*] the littoral.

None of that stops what I said about the unconscious, sticking with that, from taking precedence all the same; for otherwise, what I propose would have no meaning whatsoever. It remains to be seen how the unconscious – which I say is the effect of language, since the unconscious presupposes language's structure as necessary and sufficient – commands the function of the letter.

The fact that the letter is an instrument that is suitable for the inscription of discourse does not render it in any way unsuitable to serve the purposes to which I put it when, for example, in "The Instance of the Letter," which I mentioned earlier, I use it to show the play of what a certain Jean Tardieu calls "one word taken for another," or even "one word taken by another" – in other words, metaphor and metonymy as effects of a sentence. The letter thus easily symbolizes all signifying effects; yet this does not in any way require that the effects I use the letter as an instrument to achieve be primary [or: initial (or prior), *primaire*]. It is less important to examine this primacy [or: priority (or precedence), *primarité*], which must not even be presumed, than what it is in language that summons the littoral to the literal.

Nothing of what I wrote, with the help of letters, regarding unconscious formations – in order to rehabilitate [or: co-opt, *récupérer*] Freud's simple formulation of them as linguistic effects – allows one to confuse, as has been done, the letter with the signifier [see *Écrits*, pp. 428–29]. The unconscious formations that I inscribed with the help of letters do not authorize us to make the letter into a signifier or, still less, to assign it primacy with regard to the signifier.

Such confusion could only arise from a discourse that imports my work [or: is of concern to me, *m'importe*], a different discourse that I label "university discourse" – namely, as I have stressed sufficiently over the past year and a half, I think, knowledge put to use on the basis of semblance.

Even the slightest experience of what I deal with [or: remedy (in analyses), *à quoi je pare*] can only be situated on the basis of another discourse than that one. I should have held on to [or: protected, *gardé*] the product of the discourse that I will not designate any further, without claiming ownership thereof. It was spared, thank God. The fact remains that by importing my work [or: being of concern to me, *m'importer*], in the sense I just mentioned, people importune me.

Even if I had considered valid all of the models Freud provides in his "Project for a Scientific Psychology," where he describes the breaching or drilling of impressive [or: impressionable, *impressives*] circuits, I still would have not adopted the metaphor of writing. For it is precisely with regard to writing that I do not find his "Project" valid. Writing is not impression, regardless of all the blah blah blah about the famous *Wunderblock* [Mystic Writing Pad].

When I draw on Freud's fifty-second letter to Wilhelm Fliess, it is in order to read what Freud was able to state using the term that he forges – Wz, for *Wahrnehmungszeichen* ["indication (or sign) of perception"] – and to note that it is what he was able to find that came closest to the term "signifier" at a time when Saussure had not yet brought it back to our attention ("signifier" not being Saussure's own term, since it dates back to the Stoics [*signans*]). The fact that Freud writes it with two letters, *W* and *z*, I myself writing it with but one, S, in no way proves that the letter is primary.

Today I am thus going to try to indicate to you the crux of what I think produces the letter as a consequence, as a consequence of language, precisely on the basis of what I say: that whoever speaks inhabits it.

I will borrow its traits from something that – based on an economy of language – allows us to trace out what is being fostered by the fact that literature is, in my view, perhaps in the process of swerving toward *lituraterre.*

Don't be surprised if you see me proceed on the basis of a literal demonstration, for that is to advance in lockstep with the question itself. One might perhaps see asserted in it what the kind of demonstration that I call literary can be. I'm always a bit on the fence. Why not go for it this time?

I have just returned from a trip that I had been planning to take to Japan, owing to the littoral that I experienced during a first trip. On the basis of what I said earlier about the *Umwelt* – which I repudiated, precisely because it makes the trip impossible – you can understand that, if you follow my formulations, this ensures that it is real. Yet that would be premature. It is the parting [*départ*] that it makes impossible, apart from singing *Partons, partons*, "Let us leave, let us leave." And that happens a lot.

I will mention only one facet of this trip, something I gleaned from a new route. I just so happened to take this specific route this time, it having been quite simply prohibited the first time I went to Japan. I have to admit that it was not on the way there – along the Arctic Circle, which is the route the plane follows – that I read something. What? What I could see of the Siberian plain.

I am in the process of providing you an essay on *sibériéthique* [a condensation of "Siberia" and "ethics" (along, perhaps, with a hint of "cybernetics")]. It would not have seen the light of day if the Soviets' mistrust, not of me, but of planes, had allowed me to see the industries and military installations that make Siberia so important. Their mistrust is, therefore, what I will call an "accidental" condition. Why not even call it "occidental" [*occidentelle*], if we add a dash of murder [*occire*] to it. The buildup [*amoncellement*] of the Siberian South is what we have coming to us.

The only decisive condition here is the littoral condition, which for me, because I am a little hard of hearing, played its part only on my way back to France. For Japan, with its letters, literally tickled me a bit too much, no doubt – which was just enough for me to feel it. I am saying that I felt it because I had, of course, already situated and anticipated it here when I spoke to you a tad about the Japanese language and what constitutes it, strictly speaking [in Chapter V]. I already told you that it is writing that does so.

For that, it was undoubtedly necessary that the little "too much" I needed of what is known as art represent something. This owes to the fact that Japanese painting demonstrates that it is wedded to the letter, quite precisely in the form of calligraphy. I am fascinated by the things that hang – *kakemono*, that's how it's pronounced – on the wall of every museum over there, bearing written characters that are of Chinese extraction. I am a bit familiar with them, the tiniest little bit. Yet, however little I am familiar with them, I can gauge which of their facets are elided in cursive writing, where the singularity of the hand crushes the universal – namely, precisely what I teach you is of value only on the basis of the signifier. Do you recall what I said? All lines are vertical. That is still true even when there are no lines.

I can't make out the characters in cursive writing because I am a novice. But that is not what is important, for what I am calling singularity can prop up a more solid form. What it adds there is what is important. It is a dimension – or as I taught you to play on it, a *demansion* – in which what I already presented in my last or penultimate class resides: a word that I write, in order to have fun, the *papeludun* [a near homonym of *pas-plus-d'un*, no-more-than-one].

This is the "demansion" which, as you know, allows me (I'm not going to go back over all of that, the little mathematical game invented by Peano, etc., and the way Frege has to approach things in order to reduce the series of natural numbers, in quotes, to logic) to instate the subject in what, today again, I am going to call – since I create literature, and since I am in a good mood, as you will see, I wrote it in another form recently – the *Hun-En-Peluce* [a near homonym of *un-en-plus*, one-extra, and evoking *peluche*, stuffed animal]. That allows us to do a lot. It takes the place of what I call the *Achose* with a capital *A*, and it plugs it up with little *a*. It is perhaps no accident that little *a* can be reduced to a letter, as I designate it. At the level of calligraphy, this letter constitutes the stakes of a wager. Which wager? A wager that can be won with ink and brush.

This is how something invincibly appeared to me – in a circumstance worth recalling (namely, between the clouds) – that something being the runoff [or: surface flow, *ruissellement*], which is the only trace that appears to operate on, even more than indicate, 121 the topography in this latitude of what is known as the Siberian plain. That plain is truly desolate, in the strict sense of the term, having no vegetation; it merely reflects this runoff, and forces into the shadows whatever does not reflect.

What is runoff? It is a bouquet, a bouquet composed of what I distinguished as the first trait and what effaces it. I said this back in the day, but people always forget a part of it. Regarding the unary trait, I said that the subject is designated by the effacing of the trait. This thus occurs in two stages. The crossing out [or: effacing (or scratching out), *rature*] must thus be distinguished therein.

Litura, lituraterre. What constitutes the ground [*terre*] of the littoral is the crossing out of any trace that may have been there before. *Litura pure* is the literal. To produce this crossing out there is to reproduce the half owing to which the subject subsists. Those of you who have been here for a while – there must be fewer and fewer of you – should recall that one day I narrated the adventures of half a chicken. Only calligraphy manages to produce the definitive crossing out. You can always try to simply do what I will not do – because I would botch it up, first of all, because I don't have a brush – which is to try to make this horizontal line [*barre*], which is drawn from left to right, in order to depict the unary one as a character with a single bold stroke. It takes a long time to learn how much pressure to put on the brush [or: how to "attack" it] and how to taper it, such that what you produce will be pitiful – it is hopeless for a "wounded Westerner" [*occidenté*, combining *occidental* (Westerner) and *accidenté* (someone who was in an accident)].

You need a rapidity that can only be learned [or: a different train that can only be caught, *un train différent qui ne s'attrape*] by detaching yourself from anything that crosses you out [or: scratches you, *vous raye*].

Between center and absence, between knowledge and jouissance, there is the littoral that swerves toward the literal only if you can navigate the curve in the same way at every moment. It is on that basis alone that you can take yourself to be the agent who sustains this.

What is revealed by my vision of runoff, insofar as it is the crossing out [*rature*] that dominates there, is that by appearing between the clouds, it commingles with its source. Aristophanes summons me to find the status of the signifier – namely, semblance par excellence – in the clouds, assuming it is on the basis of their opening up [*rupture*] that this effect rains down, precipitation flowing from what had been suspended there.

It must be said that clouds are plentiful in Japanese paintings – which, as I said earlier, are thoroughly enmeshed with calligraphy.

122 It was because I was in a plane over the Siberian plain at the time that I truly grasped the function of the golden clouds that literally cover over a portion of the scenes depicted in those paintings. They unfold in a different direction than the *kakemono* – they are known as *makimono*, and they preside over the arrangement of the little scenes. Why? How can it be that people who know how to draw feel a need to combine them with these masses of clouds, unless that is precisely what introduces the signifying dimension?

The letter that constitutes a crossing out [*rature*] is thus distinguished from the signifier by the fact that it ruptures [or: bursts opens, *rupture*] semblance, dissolving what constituted form, phenomenon, and meteor. As I already told you, this is what science most palpably does at the outset regarding perceptible forms. But at the same time, this must also involve dismissing the jouissance that stems from this bursting – in other words, dissipating what it sustains by way of jouissance with this hypothesis, to put it thus [or: dissipating the hypothesis, to put it thus, of jouissance that it champions, *d'en dissiper ce qu'elle soutient de cette hypothèse, pour m'exprimer ainsi, de la jouissance*], which, in short, constitutes the world. For to have an idea of the world is to believe that it is made of drives such that life, too, is composed of them.

Well, the jouissance that is evoked when semblance bursts open is what presents itself as erosion [or: gullying (or the forming of ravines or wearing away), *ravinement*] in the real [or: in reality, *réel*] – that's the important point, in the real.

This is to define for you how writing can be called the erosion of the signified in the real – namely, the semblance that has rained down [or: pleased us, *plu*] insofar as it is what constitutes the signified. Writing does not trace the signifier. Writing harkens back [*remonte*] to the signifier only insofar as it gets its name from it, but in exactly the same way as happens to all things that are named by the signifying battery after it has enumerated them.

As I am, naturally, not sure that you understand what I am saying, I am going to have to pin this down with an opposition. Writing – the letter, that is – is in the real, and the signifier is in the symbolic. That's something you can play over and over in your heads.

I'm going to move on now to something that occurred to me later while on the plane. I mentioned that this was during my trip back to France. What was striking was to see appear other traces that resemble isobars [i.e., isopleths or isolines: curves connecting points of equal elevation]. Obviously, traces that are akin to embankments [or: backfill, *remblai*], isobars in short, are perpendicular to the traces by which the slope, that one may call supreme, of the topography is marked by curves.

They were very clear from where I was sitting. I had already seen in Osaka how the highways appear to descend from the sky. Only there could they be laid out like that, one on top of the other. The most modern Japanese architecture knows very well how to join forces with the old. Japanese architecture consists, essentially, in the beating of a bird's wing. That helped me to immediately understand that no one would ever see the shortest route between two points were it not for clouds that clearly look like roads. Nothing in the world ever follows a straight line, neither man, nor amoeba, neither fly, nor branch – nada. According to the latest studies, we know that not even light travels in a straight line, following instead the curvature of the universe.

And yet a straight line still inscribes something. It inscribes distance. But according to Newton's law, distance is absolutely nothing but an effective factor of what we call a cascading dynamic, which is such that anything that falls traces out a parabola.

Straight lines are thus only found in writing, and land surveying [*arpentage*] is based only on the sky.

But the two points that determine a straight line are artifacts because they inhabit language alone. We must not forget that our science operates only on the basis of a stream [or: runoff] of little letters and combined graphics.

"*Sous le pont Mirabeau*" ["Under the Mirabeau bridge," the beginning of the poem *Le pont Mirabeau* by Guillaume Apollinaire] – like under the bridge of a journal I ran, on the cover of which I had stuck an ear bridge, borrowed from Horus Apollo, as a billboard – "*Sous le pont Mirabeau coule la Seine*" *primitive* ["Under the Mirabeau bridge flows the" primal Seine/scene; *Seine* and *scène* are homonyms in French]. Let us not forget that it is a scene such that, if we reread Freud's case of the Wolfman, the Roman numeral V of five o'clock can ring out there [or: beat (like wings), *battre*]. But we can only enjoy this via interpretation.

The fact that the symptom establishes the order that justifies our politics – this is the step our politics has taken – implies, on the other hand, that everything about this order which is articulated can be interpreted. This is why politics is rightly placed under psychoanalysis's oversight. This might not be very comfortable for politics, as we have known it up until now, were psychoanalysis to prove more astute.

It would perhaps suffice – to place our hope in something else, as my men of letters do, if I can turn them into my companions – that we do something with writing other than create a forum [*tribune*] or a tribunal, so that other words paying tribute to ourselves [or: other words that make us into their tribute, *d'autres paroles à nous en faire nous-mêmes le tribut*] can be heard there.

124   As I have said, and never forget, there's no such thing as a metalanguage. Any logic that begins, which no logic has ever failed to do heretofore, with an object-language is skewed. Hence, there's no such thing as a metalanguage, yet the writing that is fabricated on the basis of language could, perhaps, provide material that is strong enough to change what we say [or: our intentions, *nos propos*]. I don't see any other hope for those who currently write.

Is it possible to constitute, using the littoral, a discourse that is characterized as not a semblance [or: as not based on semblance]? That is the question I am raising this year. This question obviously only arises owing to literature known as avant-garde, which is itself littoral, and thus is not propped up by semblance. Yet that does not prove anything, except to show the break that only a discourse can produce. I say "produce," bring to the fore with an effect of production – that is the schema of my quadripods from last year.

What a certain literature, that I label with the term *lituraterrir* [condensing literature with *atterrir* (to land, touch down, or wind up)], ambitiously seems to claim is that it is organized on the basis of a movement it calls scientific. It is a fact that writing has worked miracles in science, and everything suggests that these miracles are not about to cease. Nevertheless, physicists are going to be forced to take up the examination of symptoms – owing, effectively, to pollution. There are scientists who have already become attuned to symptoms, because of the polluting of the earth – now uncritically referred to as the "environment." The latter is Uexküll's idea, *Umwelt*, but "behaviorized" – in other words, completely cretinized.

To *lituraterrir* myself, I would point out that the "erosion" I have proffered here is an image, certainly, but no metaphor – writing is this erosion. But that applies to what I have just written, too. When I speak of jouissance, I legitimately invoke the audience I accumulate, and no less naturally, the jouissance [or: audience] of which I deprive myself. Your numbers keep me busy. I am prepared for them to erode.

Moving on, note that what is important about the fact that writing affects the way Japanese is spoken is that it offers us plentiful examples of *lituraterring*.

What is crucial is that writing's effect remains attached to writing, and that what transmits writing's effect is a specialized writing there

– for in Japanese this specialized writing can be read using two different pronunciations. In *onyomi* – I am not pulling the wool over your eyes, I will pronounce as little Japanese as possible – the strictly phonetic pronunciation of characters is distinct from the pronunciation provided in *kunyomi*, which is the way you say in Japanese what the character means.

But you are, naturally, going to get this all wrong. Under the pretext that the character is a letter, you are going to believe that I am telling you that in Japanese, the flotsam and jetsam of the signifier float down the river of the signified. Yet it is the letter, not the sign, that serves here as a prop for the signifier. Like anything else that follows the law of metaphor (regarding which I recently reminded you that it is the essence of language), it is always from somewhere other than where language is – namely, from discourse – that it catches anything at all in the signifier's net, i.e., writing itself.

Yet writing is promoted from there to the function of a referent, as essential as anything else, and that is what changes the status of the subject. This is why he derives his fundamental identification from a sky full of constellations, and not just from the unary trait. Well, the fact is that there are too many things propping him up, which is tantamount to there being none. This is why he relies on something else: the *Tu*. For in Japanese, there are myriad grammatical forms for even the slightest statement. There are more or less polite ways to say something, it doesn't matter what, depending on how I involve the *Tu* in it – I do so if I am Japanese. As I am not, I don't do so, for that would wear me out.

When you realize – and anyone can learn Japanese – that the slightest thing there is subject to variations in the statement, which are variations of politeness, you will have learned something. You will have learned that in Japanese, truth reinforces the fictional structure that I detect in it, by adding laws of politeness to it.

Oddly enough, that seems to imply that there is nothing repressed to defend [or: nothing to defend from repression, *il n'y ait rien à défendre du refoulé*], because the repressed itself manages to inhabit this reference to the letter. In other words, the subject is divided by language, but one of his registers can content itself with [or: confine itself to] the reference to writing, and the other with the exercise of speech.

This is undoubtedly what gave my dear friend Roland Barthes the drunken feeling that the Japanese subject, with all his good manners, serves as an envelope for nothing. This is, at least, what he says, and I recommend you have a look at his sensational book, *Empire of Signs* [New York: Hill and Wang, 1982], as he entitled it. People often make improper use of terms in their book titles. They do so for publishers. He obviously means that it is the empire of semblance. You will see that if you read the text.

I have been told that the mythical Japanese person, the Japanese man in the street, finds it awful – at least that's what I heard over there. And, indeed, however excellent Roland Barthes' text may be, I would counter his argument with what I am saying today: namely, that nothing is more distinct from the void [or: gap, *vide*] hollowed out by writing than semblance, insofar as, primo, that void is the first of my buckets that is always ready to collect jouissance, or at least invoke it by way of its artifice. Given our habits, nothing communicates less about itself than a subject who, in the final analysis, hides nothing. He need but manipulate you, and I assure you that he doesn't stop himself from doing so. To me, that is marvelous. I adore it. You are just another element of the ceremonial, in which the subject composes himself, precisely because he is able to decompose himself.

Some of you perhaps saw the *bunraku* a while back when they came to Paris. I went to see them again in Japan, having already seen them once before. The mainspring of *bunraku* is that it reveals the altogether ordinary structure of those to whom it provides their very mores. As you know, we see quite clearly, alongside the puppets, the people who are operating them. Similarly, just as in *bunraku*, everything that is said in a Japanese conversation could be read by a narrator.

That is what Barthes must have found relieving. Japan is a place where it is quite natural to rely on an interpreter. People are very happy to hire an interpreter. It doesn't require any interpretation at all. You can imagine how relieved I was. Japanese is perpetual translation turned into language.

What I like is that the only communication that I had there – apart from that with Europeans, naturally, with whom I know how to get along, according to our usual misunderstandings – with a Japanese person is also the only one that, there as elsewhere, can constitute communication, not being a dialogue – it was scientific communication.

I went to see an eminent biologist – whose name I will not mention, owing to the rules of Japanese etiquette – and that led him to show me his work, where it happens: on the blackboard, naturally. The fact that I didn't understand anything, owing to inadequate background information, in no way stopped what he wrote, his formulas, from being entirely valid for the molecules in question. My descendants will become subjects of those molecules, without me ever having had to know how I would transmit to them what made it seem plausible to classify them, like myself, as living beings.

An ascesis of writing detracts nothing from the advantages that stem from literary criticism. To come full circle regarding something more coherent, it seems to me that, owing to what I have already proposed, literary criticism cannot be considered credible unless it connects up with the impossible "it is written" with which the relationship between the sexes may someday be established.

May 12, 1971

VIII

MAN, WOMAN, AND LOGIC

The shadow of the Enlightenment
The relationship between the sexes is impossible to write
An attempt at a logical formula for man
An attempt at another formula for woman
Introducing the *hommoinzin*

Were I to abruptly begin with what I have to tell you, it might be expressed as follows.

We are exploring things on the basis of a certain discourse, mine in this case – mine insofar as it is the analyst's discourse. Let us say that this discourse determines functions. In other words, functions are determined only on the basis of a certain discourse. And it is at the level of functions determined by a certain discourse that I can establish an equivalence between writing and jouissance.

This can only be situated, naturally, within a first articulation of the functions determined by a discourse. Let's say that these terms hold the exact same place within these functions.

Why am I saying this so abruptly? So that you will put it to the test. You will see that this always leads somewhere, preferably to something precise.

This does not dispense me, of course, from taking the trouble to present it to you by suitable pathways – namely (not those that justify it for me, given the place from which I speak to you, but), those by which it can be explained.

I assume – well, I don't necessarily – that I am always addressing analysts here. This is, moreover, what makes it such that my discourse is not always easy to follow. That's because when it comes to the analyst's discourse, there is something that creates an obstacle to a certain type of inscription.

And yet I am proposing just such an inscription. It will bring us, 130 I hope, to a point from which analytic discourse will get a new lease on life, so to speak.

1

My goal is to convey to you how the transmission of a letter is related to something essential and fundamental in the organization of any discourse – namely, jouissance.

To do so, I must set the tone on each occasion. How could I do so if I didn't remind you of the basic example with which I began?

We must explicitly study the letter as such, insofar as it has a feminizing effect, as I said. That is how I began my *Écrits*. The letter in "The Purloined Letter," as I again stressed last time, functions as it does because no one knows its contents, and because, in the final analysis, no one will know anything about them right to the end.

The letter in question is quite exemplary. Naturally, only a simpleton would think – and even then, I believe that not even a simpleton would have thought this – that it was something as crude as a message attesting to what is commonly known as a sexual relationship, although it was written by a man – as Poe tells us, and it is emphasized there, by a high-ranking man – to a Queen. That is obviously not what creates the drama there. A Court – in other words, something founded on the distribution of jouissance, which is the best definition we can provide of a Court – operates in such a way that, in this distribution, sexual relationships are put in their rightful place: the lowest place possible, obviously. No one considers services of this ilk that a grand lady may receive from a lackey to be noteworthy.

Naturally, when it comes to the Queen, and precisely because she is the Queen, things take on a different complexion. But it is crystal clear – first of all, and this stems from experience – that a well-bred man is one who, as it were, because of his noble birth, could never feel slighted by a liaison on his wife's part, assuming it is carried out with propriety. The only thing that could mar this picture is, of course, the entry of bastards into his lineage; but that can, nevertheless, serve to rejuvenate an old bloodline. Even though we don't see much of this in our times, this framework is nevertheless exemplary and fundamental when we examine [or: account for, *raisonner*] social relationships.

It can be clearly seen here that nothing reveals the element that must apparently be irreducible in reality – namely, the function of need – like an order founded on artifice. I told you that there is an order in which the following is thoroughly put in its place: the fact that a subject, no matter how high-ranking he may be, reserves that portion of irreducible jouissance for himself, the minimal part that cannot be sublimated, as Freud expressly puts it. Only an order founded on artifacts – I mentioned a Court, inasmuch as it adds

the artifact of nobility to a second artifact, that of an ordered distribution of jouissance – can put need in its proper place. The need
explicitly specified as such is sexual need.

Yet, if, on the one hand, the artifact satisfies a certain theorization that seems to specify that the relationship between the sexes
is natural – this is an elementary theorization, which is, in short,
biological – basing, as it does, on a need, what must result from it
(viz., reproduction), we observe, on the other hand, that it obviously
leaves room for the possibility that reproduction may not be legitimate, in quotes.

We can obviously admit that this need – this irreducible thing
in the relationship between the sexes – always exists, and Freud
says as much. What is clear is that it is not measurable – at least,
it can only be measured in the artifact, the artifact of the relation
to the Other with a capital *O*. It is not measurable, and it is clearly
this indeterminacy that indicates what is fundamental – namely,
that the sexual relationship cannot be inscribed or *grounded* qua
relationship.

This is why the letter with which I opened my *Écrits* is designated
by what it is, and by the fact that it indicates everything Freud
himself articulated: if it serves some sexual purpose, it is certainly
not that of a sexual relationship, but of a relationship that is, let us
say, sexed [*sexué*]. The difference between the two is as follows:

What Freud demonstrated, what he contributed that is decisive,
is that, via the unconscious, we glimpse that everything having to
do with language is related to sex – everything having to do with
language bears a certain relation to sex – precisely insofar as the
relationship between the sexes cannot in any way be inscribed in
language, at least at present.

The so-called sexualization that Freud's doctrine supposedly   132
accomplishes of what one might call "subjective functions," assuming we situate them as linguistic, essentially consists in the fact that
what should result from language – namely, that the sexual relation
can somehow be inscribed in it – utterly fails, as we see all the time.
It cannot be inscribed.

We already see here the functioning of something that is part
of this effect of a gap or division, which is the one we deal with
regularly – indeed always – and this is why I must in some sense
train you in it. People think, for example, that I have said that the
relationship between the sexes fails to be enunciated in language.
But what I have said is not "enunciated" but rather "inscribable."
If I say "inscribable," it is because what is required for there to be a
function is that something be producible through language, which
is the explicit writing of a function. Namely, something that I have

already more than once symbolized in the simplest way: F in a certain relationship with x – namely, $F(x)$.

Therefore, when we say that language does not account for the relationship between the sexes, let us ask ourselves in exactly what respect it does not account for it. It does not account for it insofar as it cannot make it such that the inscription it can provide is what I define as the *actual* inscription of what a sexual relationship would be. The latter is something that would connect the two poles – the two terms known as "man" and "woman," insofar as this man and this woman are of sexes specified as male and female, respectively – in whom? In beings who speak, in other words, who, inhabiting language as they do, turn out to derive therefrom the habit of speaking.

Giving precedence to the letter in woman's relationship to something – something that, owing to written law, is inscribed in the context in which the thing takes place, by virtue of the fact that she is, as a Queen, the very image of woman, as the King's spouse – is noteworthy. Something is improperly symbolized here and, as usual, around the relationship qua sexual; it is no wonder that it can only be incarnated in fictional beings.

It is in this context that the fact that a letter is addressed to her takes on the value that I designate: that of a sign. To cite myself: "For this sign," I wrote regarding the letter, "is clearly that of woman, because she brings out her very being therein by founding it outside the law, which ever contains her – due to the effect of origins – in a position as signifier, nay, as fetish" [*Écrits*, p. 22]. It is obvious that such an enunciation – which is, nevertheless, the one from which, I would say, the women's movement stems, and which says that the law always contains her, owing to the effect of her origins, in a signifying position, or even as a fetish – cannot be proffered anywhere other than in psychoanalysis.

It is inasmuch as the relationship between the sexes is, as it were, "state-ified" – in other words, incarnated in the relationship between the King and Queen, highlighting truth's fictional structure – that the letter in fact fulfills its function. The letter is surely posited as being related to the marked deficiency of a certain promoting (which is in some sense arbitrary and fictional) of the relationship between the sexes. It is there that the letter, taking on its value, raises a question.

This gives me the opportunity to underscore something. Don't think that this is going to connect up in some direct way with what I just reminded you of, but keep in mind that these kinds of jumps or shifts are necessitated by the point to which I wish to lead you. It is an opportunity to note that, the fact that the truth advances only on the basis of a fictional structure is confirmed here. It is because a fictional structure is promoted somewhere, which is the very essence of language, that something can be produced: a sort of questioning, pushing, or squeezing that forces truth into a corner, so to speak, requiring it to undergo verification. This is nothing but the dimension of science.

The pathway by which we see science advancing is justified, as it were, by the fact that logic's share in it is considerable. Regardless of the originally and fundamentally fictional character of what constitutes the material with which language works, it is clear that there is a pathway of verification which is committed to grasping where fiction comes up short, as it were, and to grasping what stops it. Regardless of what has allowed us to inscribe – and you will see what that means later – the progress of logic, I mean, the written pathway by which it has advanced, it is clear that what makes fiction come up short is altogether effective, being inscribed right at the core of the fictional system. It is known as contradiction.

If science has apparently made progress by pathways other than those of tautology, this in no way affects the import of my comment – namely, that it is precisely because truth was summoned (and this summons was brought to bear from a certain point) to be verifiable that science was forced to abandon all sorts of other, supposedly 134 intuitive premises. I have sufficiently emphasized the nature of everything that paved the way for Newton's discovery, for example. No fiction could prove satisfying, if not one among them that had to abandon all recourse to intuition in order to confine itself to something inscribable. This is why we have to hold to the inscribable in its relationship to verification.

What, in a nutshell, did I say about the effect of the letter in "The Purloined Letter"? That it feminizes those who find themselves in a certain position, which is that of being in its shadow.

We see here the importance of the function of shadows. Last time already, in what I told you about what a written text is – I mean, about something that is presented in a literal or literary form – I mentioned that there must be a source of light for a shadow to be produced. Right. But you didn't seem to notice that, because of this, the *Aufklärung* [the Enlightenment] involves something that maintains a fictional structure. I am talking about the historical era, which was no mere flash in the pan. It can be of use to us (as in this case, and that's what I am doing) to retrace its pathways, or to take them up anew. What creates light begins from the field that is itself defined as being that of truth. Now, even if it were to have an efficient effect on what constitutes opacity, the actual light that this field gives off at every moment casts a shadow, and it is the shadow that has an impact. This is why we always have to investigate truth itself regarding its fictional structure.

This is why, in the final analysis, it turns out (as is expressly stated in the text) that the letter does not satisfy the woman to whom it is addressed by arriving at its destination, but the subject – namely, to redefine the subject, that which is divided in fantasy – in other words, reality qua generated by a fictional structure.

That is how the story ends – at least in a second text, which is mine. We must start there if we are to further investigate the nature of the letter. To the degree to which this has never been done before, I must, in order to do so, similarly prolong/purloin [cf. the etymology of "purloin" and *Écrits*, pp. 20–21] this discourse on the letter.

Voilà.

2

We must begin with the following: there's a reason why I ask you to overlook nothing that is produced in the realm of logic.

It is certainly not to make you force yourselves, as it were, to keep up with all of its constructions and byways. The deficit of any and all possibility of reflection appears nowhere better than in the constructions that go by the self-assigned heading of "symbolic logic." I mean that nothing is more awkward – this is well known, right? – than the introduction to a treatise on logic.

Logic's inability to establish itself on a firm footing is quite striking. This is why I recommend you read these treatises. The more modern they are – the more they are at the cusp of progress in logic, progress in the inscription of what is known as logical articulation – the more fascinating they are. Logic is incapable of defining itself, its goals, its principle, or anything even vaguely resembling a subject matter. This is quite strange, which is why it is highly suggestive.

It is worth touching on and exploring the status of something that can be situated, assuredly, only on the basis of language. We may perhaps be able to grasp here why whatever is proposed (always awkwardly) in this language as involving, let's say, a correct usage of this language, can only be enunciated as not being able to justify itself – or being able to justify itself only in the most confused way, by all sorts of attempts, which consist, for example, in dividing language into an object-language and a metalanguage, which is exactly the opposite of what is demonstrated by the fact that there is no way to speak, even for an instant, about this supposed object-language without using, not a metalanguage, but everyday language. We can see in this very failure the status of an articulation that is closely related to the functioning of language – in other words, the following articulation: the relationship between the sexes cannot be written.

On this topic, and solely in order to take a few steps that recall [136] to mind the dimension in which we are working, I will remind you how what inaugurates the trajectory of logic presents itself at first – namely, as formal logic in Aristotle's work.

I am not going to present his *Prior Analytics* to you, even if it might be very instructive. Each of you can take the trouble to read his text. Should you put yourself to the test of rereading it, you will see there what a syllogism is. We must begin from syllogisms, at least that's where I will begin, since I ended on them at our second-to-last meeting.

I do not wish to take them up here by exemplifying every form of syllogism, as we are limited by time. Let it suffice to quickly highlight the status of the universal and the particular in their affirmative forms alone.

I am going to discuss the syllogism known as *darii*, which includes a universal affirmative and two particulars, and remind you what arises from a certain way of presenting things. Nothing can function here unless, in the fabric of discourse, we replace a signifier by a hole, as it were, a hole made by replacing that signifier with a letter. If, borrowing Aristotle's terms, we say "Every man is good," "Every man" [*Tout homme*] is the universal; and I have said enough to prepare you to grasp that there need not exist any men for the universal to hold up. "Every man is good" can mean that there are only good men, that whatever is not good is not man. The second articulation, which is known as "the minor premise," is "Some animals are men." The third articulation, known as the conclusion, is "Some animals are thus good."

It is clear that this holds up only owing to the use of the letter. This is because, if they are not propped up by a letter, there is no equivalence between "man" – the subject of the universal in "Every man" – which plays the role here of what is known as the "middle term," and the same middle term in the place where it is used as an attribute – namely, in the proposition "Some animals are men." This distinction, which is worth making, in fact requires a great deal of care.

The "man" in "Every man," when he is the subject, implies the function of a universal that gives him his symbolic status as sole prop – namely, that something can be called "man." In the form of [137] an attribute, and in order to maintain that some animals are men, we must state that what we call "man" in the animal kingdom is the type of animal that happens to inhabit language, for this is the only thing that distinguishes men from other animals. At that point, we can justifiably posit that man is good. It is a limitation.

What can, in fact, establish that man is good? It was brought out long ago, before Aristotle's time, that the idea of the "good" [*bon*] can only be established on the basis of language. For Plato, on the other hand, the Ideas are at the very root of language. Since, to his way of thinking, language is the world of Ideas, there is no language or possible articulation without the elementary [*primaire*] Idea of the good [*bien*].

It is altogether possible to investigate the status of the "good" in language differently. You simply deduce the consequences that result, as concerns the universal, from the fact that man is good. As you know, that's what Mencius – who I did not mention for no reason in my recent lectures – did.

What does "good" mean? Good for what? Or is it simply to say, as people have been saying for some time, "You are good"? If this change in accent has occurred regarding the use of the word "good," it is perhaps because we have arrived at a specific point in the calling into question of truth, as well as of discourse. There's no need to specify what it's good for. To say it's fit [*bon*] for military purposes or fit to be sent to the front lines is saying too much. "You are good" has an absolute value. In fact, it is the central bond between the good and discourse. Once you inhabit a certain type of discourse, you are fit to be commanded by it.

This is why we are led to the function of the master signifier, about which I stressed that it is not in and of itself inherent in language, and that language makes possible only a set number of discourses. Of those that I specifically outlined last year at least, none eliminates the function of the master signifier.

Under such conditions, to say that "Some animals are good" is obviously not a simply formal conclusion. This is why I stressed earlier that the use of logic, regardless of what it itself may say, must in no wise be reduced to tautology. The notion that some animals are good is not limited to those who are men, as is implied by the existence of domestic animals, as they are known. It is no accident that I emphasized a while back that we cannot say that domestic animals have no familiarity with speech [*usage de la parole*]. While they do not dispose of language, much less the resources of discourse, they are nevertheless subject to speech. This is even what distinguishes them from other animals and makes them into a means of production.

As you see, this opens a door that will take us a little bit further. Let me point out that women are associated with such animals in the Ten Commandments: "Thou shall not covet thy neighbor's wife, nor his ox, nor his ass." We have here a precise enumeration of the means of production. I'm not saying this to give you an occasion to snicker, but to reflect by relating what I am pointing out here in passing to what I previously said about what is expressed in the Ten Commandments – namely, nothing other than the laws of speech. This limits their interest. But it is very important to limit the interest of things in order to know why they hit home.

Having said that as best I could, my word – that is, by a pathway that is, as usual, the one I am obliged to take, like the upside down A, the buffalo head, ∀ – I will now move onto the next step, the one allowed by the progress of logical inscription.

You know that something quite beautiful happened. Somewhere around two thousand years after the first attempt was made by making holes in the right place – namely, by replacing terms with letters (terms known as "extreme" and "mean," the terms known as "major" and "minor" being propositions) – the attempt was reinscribed [or: written differently]. You are aware that, thanks to the logic inaugurated by Morgan and Boole – simply inaugurated by them, for it was not taken to its final stage by them – we arrived at formulas involving quantifiers.

I am going to quickly write on the blackboard and then I'll be back.

Figure 8.1 Distribution of the Quantifiers

I added little circles to this figure to make it clear that the bar does not separate the two F(x)s, which would mean absolutely nothing, but that it relates solely to the F(x) written below it and signifies the negation of F(x). It's later than I thought, which may require me to abbreviate a little.

It is owing to the progress of mathematics – mathematics having managed to be completely written, thanks to algebra – that people could imagine using letters to do something other than make holes. They imagined using them to write our four types of propositions differently, the four that revolve around "every" and "some," words that give rise to ambiguities, as I could easily show you. The operation of complete inscription allowed people, consequently, to consider and write that what at first presented itself as a subject could be taken as equivalent to "every x," on condition that we assign it this upside-down A, and that we thus needed to know to what extent a certain "every x" could satisfy a function.

I need not underscore – but I will anyway, for if I don't this might seem quite empty – that, in mathematics, this is quite meaningful. Insofar as we remain at the level of the letter, wherein lies the power of mathematics, the x on the left, insofar as it is unknown, can legitimately be posited (or not posited) as finding its place in what turns out to be the function that corresponds to it – namely, the place where the same x is taken as a variable [on the right, in $F(x)$].

To move along more quickly, as it is getting late, I will illustrate this.

I mentioned that the x on the left, the one in Vx, is an unknown. Take, for example, the root of a quadratic equation. Can I say that every root of a quadratic equation can be inscribed in the function F that defines x as a variable, this function being the one on the basis of which real numbers are established?

For those of you to whom this is truly a foreign language, let me simplify things by saying that the real numbers are all the usual numbers you know (including the irrational numbers, even if you don't know what they are). It is important to realize that people have managed to set the real numbers on a firm footing. Since you 140 haven't a clue about imaginary numbers, I am indicating this just to give you an idea that it is worth making a function out of real numbers.

Right. It is quite clear that one cannot say that every root of a quadratic equation satisfies the function by which real numbers are established, quite simply because there are roots of quadratic equations that are imaginary numbers, and the latter are not included among the real numbers.

What I want to emphasize is that with that, people think they have gone far enough. Well, they haven't. They haven't said enough about "every x" or the relationship people believe they can substitute for "some." There are roots of quadratic equations that are among the real numbers, and others that aren't. But in neither case can we see a purely formal transposition in what results therefrom, a complete homology of universals and particulars, affirmative or negative, respectively.

People say that the function is not always true. What can it mean for a function not to be true? When you write a function, it is what it is, even if it goes well beyond that of the real numbers. It means, regarding the unknown constituted by the root of the quadratic equation, that I cannot write, in order to situate it there, the function of real numbers; that is something quite different from the universal negative, whose properties were already such as to put it in abeyance, as I sufficiently stressed when I talked about it before [in Chapter VI].

The exact same thing holds true at the level of "There exists an x." There exist certain roots of the quadratic equation regarding which I can write the so-called function of real numbers by saying that they satisfy it, and there are others regarding which I cannot write the function of real numbers. This, nevertheless, does not negate the function of real numbers.

This is going to take us to the third step, to which everything I have said to you today is designed to lead us.

3

As you saw, in trusting to my memory regarding what I wanted to rearticulate, I accidentally wrote the function with the little bar above it, symbolizing something altogether different from what I actually wanted to say.

You perhaps noticed that it didn't even occur to me, at least up until now, nor to you, that the bar of negation could perhaps play a role in the column, not on the right, but on the left. Let us try it. What can we extract from this?

What can we say about the fact that the function – let us call it Φx, as if at random, while placing the bar of negation over the $\forall$, something we have never done before – would not vary? It can be spoken or written.

I will begin by speaking it: it is not with respect to every x that the function *Phi* of x, Φx, can be written:

$$\overline{\forall x}.\Phi x$$

Figure 8.2 Negation of the Universal Quantifier

It is not with respect to an existing [or: extant] x that the function *Phi* of x can be written:

$$\overline{\exists x}.\Phi x$$

Figure 8.3 Negation of the Existential Quantifier

There you have it. I have not yet said whether it is inscribable or not. But in putting it thus, I am enunciating something that depends solely on the existence of writing. In short, these two negations [the one over the quantifier and the one over the function] have nothing in common. The one over the function is such that I do not write the function; instead, I exclude it. As someone who was quite an astute grammarian put it long ago, this form of negation is "foreclusive" [Pichon]: the function shall not be written; I don't want to know anything about it. The one over the quantifier is "discordant." It is not insofar as there would be a "for every x," i.e., $\forall x$, that I can or cannot write Φx. It is not insofar as "there exists an x," i.e., $\exists x$, that I can or cannot write Φx.

142   This brings us right to the heart of the impossibility of writing the relationship between the sexes.

Well-known fictional structures regarding this relationship have existed for quite some time – those, in particular, on which all religions are based. Owing to psychoanalytic experience, we subsequently managed to establish that this relationship cannot exist without a third term, which is, strictly speaking, the phallus.

Naturally, I suspect that certain people will think that this third term takes care of everything [or: does it all, *va tout seul*]. People will say that there must be a relationship between the sexes because there is a third term. It is very difficult to provide an image of this, to show that there is something unknown, x, that is man here [see Figure 8.4], and that there is something unknown, x, that is woman on the other side, and that the third term, qua third term, is very precisely characterized by the fact that it is not a middle term [*médium*].

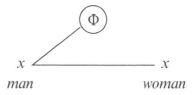

Figure 8.4 The Character of the Third Term

If we connect the third term to one of the other two terms, man, for example, we can be sure that it will not communicate with woman, and vice versa. That is the precise character of the third term.

If someone once even invented the function of attributes, why wouldn't that be related, in the first ridiculous steps of the structure of semblance, to the idea that every man is phallic and every woman is not? What we need to establish is something entirely different. It is that "some man is phallic," on the basis of the following, which is expressed in the second formula, that it is not qua particular that he is phallic.

Man is the phallic function insofar as he is "all man" [or: "all men" (or "every man"), *tout homme*]. But as you know, it is highly doubtful that the "all man" exists. That is what is at stake here: he can only be the phallus insofar as he is "allman" [*touthomme*] – in other words, nothing more than a signifier.

For women, the stakes are the exact opposite, as I told you. This is what is expressed by the discordant statement above [$\overline{\forall} x.\Phi(x)$], the one I only wrote without writing it, as it were – since I pointed out that it is a discordant statement, which is propped up only by enunciating it. It says that Woman cannot occupy her place in the relationship between the sexes, she cannot be it, except insofar as she is "a woman." As I vigorously stressed, there is no such thing as "all woman" [or: "all women" (or "every woman"), *toute femme*]. 143

What I wanted to propose and illustrate to you today is that logic bears the mark of the sexual impasse. If we follow its movement and progress in a field which seems to have no connection whatsoever with what is at stake in our experience, analytic experience, you will find the same impasses, the same obstacles, the same gaps, and, in short, the same absence of closure of a fundamental triangle [Figure 8.4].

I'm astonished that the time has flown by so quickly, given what I had to present today, and that I must now break off. Before we meet again on the second Wednesday of June, I believe that it may be easy for you to grasp the applicability of what I have presented today.

Something that results from this is, for example, that nothing related to man's status can be established – seen from the perspective of analytic experience – without artificially and mythically creating the "allman" [*touthomme*] on the basis of the presumed mythical father of *Totem and Taboo*, the one who is able to bring jouissance to all women.

But inversely, we see what results from the fact that it is only on the basis of being "*a* woman" that her status can be established in what is inscribable by not being inscribable [or: because she is not that, *de ne pas l'être*] – in other words, in what remains gaping with respect to the relationship between the sexes. Something thus happens that is legible in the oh-so-precious function of hysterics: they are the ones who speak the truth regarding the relationship between the sexes.

It is hard to imagine how psychoanalysis's path could have been blazed if we hadn't had them. To give meaning to Freud's discovery, we must set out from the fact that neurosis, or at least one of the neuroses – I will demonstrate it for the other one, too – is nothing but the strict point where the truth of a failure is articulated (which is no less true everywhere else than where truth is spoken).

What the hysteric articulates is obviously that, as regards making [or: playing the part of] the "allman," she is capable of doing so as much as the "allman" himself – namely, in her imagination. Owing to this, she doesn't need him. But if, by chance, the phallus – namely, what she thinks of herself as having been castrated of, as Freud sufficiently emphasized – is of interest [or: of concern] to her in the course of analytic treatment, she couldn't care less about it, for we mustn't believe she doesn't have access to this jouissance. If, by chance, the relationship between the sexes interests her, she must be interested in the third element, the phallus. Since she can only be interested in it via a man, and since it is not clear that there is even one [real] man, everything she does will be oriented toward what I call having "at least one."

I will end today, my goodness, on this notion of the "at least one," because our time is up. You will see that, in what follows, I will have to connect it up with what is already articulated here – namely, the function of the "*un en peluce*" [the "one-extra" or "one made of plush" (*peluche*, which also means "stuffed animal")] which, as you will note, I have not written here the way I wrote it last time [*Hun-En-Peluce*]. I didn't write it this way by chance. I believe that it may, all the same, remind a number of you of something.

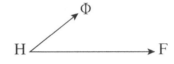

Figure 8.5 Schema of the *Hommoinzin*

I will write this "at least one" – qua essential function of the relationship, insofar as it situates woman with regard to a key ternary point, the phallic function, because its function is inaugural, inaugural of a dimension, which is the one I require for a discourse that might not be a [or: that would not be based on] semblance – as follows: *hommoinzin*.

May 19, 1971

IX

A MAN, A WOMAN, AND PSYCHOANALYSIS

{Today I am going to expand on something I took the trouble to write out [Lacan's asides are indicated in curly braces here]. I'm not saying that to all and sundry [*à la cantonade*, which includes *la . . . can* in it] just for the heck of it. It's not superfluous that I wrote.

I may perhaps drone on about something regarding the term writing [*écrit*], but if you have adequately understood what I have discussed this year regarding the function of writing, I will have no need to justify it further – if not in actual fact [or: in reality, *dans le fait*], in action. Indeed, it is not immaterial that what I am going to say to you now was written out. It doesn't have the same import at all if I say to you that "I wrote" or "I wrote this for you."}

A man and a woman can hear each other [*s'entendre*: a play on words: literally, hear or understand each other, figuratively, get along], I am not saying they can't. They can actually hear each other scream.

{This would be mere banter if I hadn't written it for you. The word "written" [*écrit*] presupposes something – something that is at least suspected by you, at least a certain number of you – that I said back in the day about the scream [Edvard Munch's "The Scream"; see Seminar XII, class given on March 17, 1965; the word *cri* (scream) is included in *écrit*]. I cannot return to that here.}

They scream at each other in cases in which they don't manage to get along in any other way – in other words, about something that is the guarantee [or: pledge, *gage*] of their entente. Such things are never lacking, including at times, and this one is the best, getting along [*entente*] in bed.

Such things are never lacking, certainly, and it is in this regard that they are lacking in something. Do men and women only get along – that is, get along qua man and qua woman, meaning sexually – when they shut up? That is out of the question, for men and women have no need to speak to be caught up in a discourse. They are actually facts [or: fabrications, *faits*] of discourse, to employ the same term I mentioned earlier.

Cracking a smile here would suffice, it seems, to hint that they are not that alone. Who wouldn't grant it? But the fact that they are also effects of discourse freezes the smile; and it is only in this way, frozen by such a remark, that the smiles found on ancient statues take on meaning. Infatuation, for its part, snickers.

Natural (as it were) male and female beings thus have to get themselves recognized [*se faire valoir*] as such in a discourse.

There is no discourse that is not about semblance [or: based on semblance, *Il n'est discours que de semblant*]. If that wasn't already perfectly obvious all by itself, I have said so, too, and will remind you how I put it. Semblance is only exposed from the standpoint of truth. Scientists, undoubtedly, never mention truth. Which is no reason for us to be more concerned about it. Truth can do just fine without us. In order for truth to make itself heard, it is enough for it to say "I speak," and we believe it because it is true. Whoever is speaking, is speaking. Nothing is of any concern – I am recalling to mind here what I said about the wager, illustrating it via Pascal [see Seminar XVI] – unless truth says it. Qua truth, it can say nothing other than semblance regarding jouissance, and it is regarding sexual jouissance that it wins every time.

{For the possible use of those who weren't here the last few times, I put back up on the blackboard the algebraic figures with which I believed I could highlight what is at stake regarding what we are forced into [*coinçage*] when we write what concerns the relationship between the sexes.

$$\overline{\forall} x.\Phi x \qquad \overline{\exists} x.\Phi x$$

Figure 9.1 Formulas for Woman and Man

It is owing to the two bars – I dub them bars of negation – placed above the symbols on the left side of each formula, $\forall$ and $\exists$, respectively, that everything that can (cor)respond to the semblance of sexual jouissance is situated, with regard to what is at stake. The two bars here are such that they must not be written, since we quite simply don't write what cannot be written.

We can say that they must not be written because it is *not* regarding "every x" [$\overline{\forall} x$] that the function Φ of x can be posited. Woman is posited on the basis of this "it is not regarding every x."

There is no x $[\overline{\exists x}]$ that satisfies the function by which the variable is defined, as being the function Φx. The status of man, of the male, I mean, is formulated on the basis of the fact that there exists no such x. But the negation here merely serves the function known as 147 *Verneinung* [negation]; in other words, it is only posited by having first proposed that "some man" exists, whereas it is with regard to "every woman" [or: "all women" (or "all woman"), *toute femme*] that a woman situates herself. This is a reminder. It was not included in what I wrote, to which I will now return.

You are right to take notes, I see that many of you are doing so. Writing's only virtue is that afterwards you can situate yourself with respect to it.}

You would do well to follow me in my discipline of names. {I will have to come back to it, especially next time, which will be the concluding class of the year.} The proper characteristic of a name [*le propre du nom*] is to be a proper noun [or: proper name, *nom propre*], even for a name that has dropped down to the level of a common noun; we wouldn't be wasting our time to refind a proper use [or: its own purpose, *un emploi propre*] for it. But when a name has remained proper enough, don't hesitate – follow my example and call the thing by its name: "The Freudian Thing," for example, as I did, {as you know, at least I like to imagine you do. I will return to this next time.

To name something is to make an appeal [or: is to call for something]. In what I wrote, too,} the thing in question, the Freudian thing, stands up and does its shtick. I am not the one who dictates its act to it. It would be quite easy – the kind of final ease in semblance toward which so many lives strive – if, as a man, male, I weren't exposed to the wind of castration. {Reread my text.}

The truth [*la vérité*] – my unfuckable partner – is certainly exposed to the same wind. She [the truth, *Elle*] even circulates it – being in fashion [literally, being in the wind, *être dans le vent*]. But she couldn't care less about this wind [literally, this wind neither cools nor warms her, *ne lui fait ni chaud ni froid*], because jouissance is not her cup of tea – she leaves jouissance to semblance [*la vérité, c'est qu'elle la laisse au semblant*].

This semblance also has a name – borrowed from eras that were mysterious simply because the Mysteries abounded then, eras at which it named the knowledge fecundity supposedly has and, as such, knowledge offered up to adoration in the guise of the semblance of an organ [see *Écrits*, p. 523].

This semblance, which is exposed by pure truth, is, we must recognize, "rather phallic" [*assez phalle*, which sounds just like *acéphale*, acephalous], rather involved in what for us is initiated by virtue of coitus – namely, the selection of genotypes, with the reproduction of the phenotype, and everything that ensues – involved enough, thus, to deserve the ancient name "phallus."

It is clear that the inheritance that it covers (over) is now reduced to the acephalous nature of this selection – that is, to the impossibility of subordinating the jouissance said to be sexual to what would *sub rosa* [secretly or confidentially] specify the choices made by men and women, who are taken to be carriers of a specific share of genotypes, since, in the best of cases, it is the phenotype that guides their choice.

In truth, and that's the word for it, a proper name – for the phallus, too, is a proper name – is stable only on a map where it designates a desert. Deserts are the only things on maps that do not change names. It is notable that even the deserts produced in the name of a religion, which are not rare, are never designated by the name of those who devastated them. A desert is only given a new name when it is fructified.

This is not the case for sexual jouissance, knowledge about which science has failed to provide, despite its advances.

It is, on the other hand, owing to the barrier that sexual jouissance constitutes to the advent of a relationship between the sexes in discourse that its place is carved out [*évidé*] there to the point of becoming obvious [*évidente*] in psychoanalysis. Such is *die Bedeutung des Phallus*, in the sense that the word *Bedeutung* has in Frege's logic.

This is why – I have my mischievous side [or: guile, *malices*] – it is in German, because I delivered the message included under this heading in my *Écrits* in Germany in honor of the centennial of Freud's birth ["The Signification of the Phallus"]. It was gratifying to see the shock it produced in a country where my message could best resound. {You can't imagine this, now that you all stroll around with a doorstop like that [the *Écrits*] under your arm. At the time, *die Bedeutung des Phallus* had an impact.} To say that I was expecting as much would be to say nothing, at least in my tongue.

My strength lies in knowing how to wait. As regards the shock in question, I am not alluding here to Germany's twenty-five years of racial cretinization. That would be to give those twenty-five years too much credit.

I would rather point out that *die Bedeutung des Phallus* is, in reality, a pleonasm. *There is no other* Bedeutung *in language than the phallus.*

In the final analysis, language, which brings things into existence, merely connotes the impossibility of symbolizing the relationship between the sexes in beings that inhabit language, owing to the fact that their ability to speak stems from this habitat. And don't forget what I said about the fact that speech is not the privilege of those who inhabit it, for they evoke speech in every creature they domi- 149 nate through the effect of discourse. {That begins with my dog, for example, the one I have been talking about for a long time, and it goes very far.}

"The eternal silence," as the man said, "of infinite spaces" will have lasted but an instant, like so many other eternities. All kinds of things speak in the realm of the new astronomy, the astronomy that began immediately after this little remark made by Pascal.

Language acquires its structure from the fact that it is constituted on the basis of a single *Bedeutung*. This structure consists in the fact that we cannot, since we inhabit it, use it except to create metaphors – from which stem all the mythical insanities by which its inhabitants live – and metonymies, from which they acquire the "scant reality" that remains to them, which takes the form of surplus jouissance.

Now, what I have just said is ratified only by history, starting with the appearance of writing, which is never just an *inscription*, even in the "audiovisual" forms of it now being promoted. Since its origins, and right up to its latest protean technical forms, writing has never been anything but what is articulated as the bone [*os*] on which language is the flesh. This is why it demonstrates that sexual jouissance has no bone(r) [*os*], we having suspected as much owing to the mores of the organ which provide, in the speaking male, its comical side.

But writing, not language, serves as the (back)bone(r) [or: hitch, *os*] of all the jouissances that, owing to discourse, turn out to be available to speaking beings. Supplying them with (back)bone, writing emphasizes what was certainly accessible, albeit masked: the relationship between the sexes is not found in the field of truth, because the discourse that establishes it is based on semblance alone – paving the way solely to jouissances that parody (that's the word for it!) the truth [*celle*] that is effective there, but that remains foreign to it.

Such is the Other of jouissance, forever inter-dic(k)ted [or: prohibited (or spoken between the lines), *inter-dit*], the one language does not allow us to inhabit, unless it is supplied with (and why not employ this image?) space suits.

{This image perhaps conveys something to you. There are some of you who are not so overly involved in unions that you can be moved by our visit to the moon.} Men have been dreaming about the moon for a long time. Now they have walked on it.

150 {To clearly grasp what this voyage means, you must do as I did before returning from Japan. Then one realizes that dreaming about the moon serves a true function. Someone – who shall remain unnamed, because I don't wish to show off my erudition here – is still locked up there. It is truly him. We realize what *persona* means – it's the very person himself, his mask,} that is locked up in a little Japanese cabinet and they show it to visitors. We know it is him [the Shogun Ashikaga Yoshimasa], and they let us see him there. That is in Kyoto, in a place that is known as the Silver Pavilion. He dreamt about the moon. We like to believe that he contemplated it rather phallically, even though that leaves us a bit flustered. We no longer grasp this very well. In order to get over our fluster, we have to realize that a footprint on the moon is tantamount to the signifier of A barred on my graph: S(A̶).

All of that is banter. Such banter signals and warns me that I am verging on structuralism. {If I am obliged to verge on it, it is not my fault, naturally.} I would blame it – but it's for you to judge – on the predicament in which I find myself and that I will label in a way that may not immediately appear clear to you, but which I will have to indicate between now and when we part in a week – in other words, the refusal to perform. It is an illness, the illness of our times, from which we all suffer, since this refusal constitutes the cult of competence – in other words, the cult of a certain ideality with which, like much of the scientific field, I am reduced, moreover, to authorizing myself before you.

The result – these are mere anecdotes – is that one of my *Écrits*, "Function and Field of Speech and Language," was published in English in a book entitled *The Language of the Self* [Baltimore, MD: Johns Hopkins University Press, 1968], and I just found out that in Spanish my work was just as freely entitled "Structuralist Aspects of Freud" [the publisher of the first Spanish edition of *Écrits* added a subtitle: *Lectura Estructuralista de Freud*, "A Structuralist Reading of Freud"]. Well, let's move on.

Competence neglects the fact that it is based on incompetence, offering itself up to be worshiped in the form of ideality. That is the way in which it makes concessions, and I am going to give you an example of this. The sentence with which I began – "A man and a woman can hear each other [or: get along], I am not saying they can't" – well, I said that to make the pill easier to swallow. But a pill like that doesn't make things any better.

Coining the term "structuralism" is an attempt to prolong the delegating – to certain specialists, specialists of truth, as was done for a while – of a certain vacuum [*vide*] that is glimpsed in the fact that jouissance is becoming scarce. 151

That is what existentialism didn't fail to notice, after phenomenology, which is far more hypocritical [or: deceitful, *faux jeton*], had thrown down the gauntlet with its breathing exercises. It occupied places left deserted by philosophy because they were not appropriate places. Currently, those places are just barely good enough for erecting a memorial to philosophy's contribution – which is no small potatoes – to the master's discourse that philosophy definitively stabilized with the help of science.

Whether we agree with Marx or not, and whether he stood philosophy on its feet or turned it on its head, it is clear that philosophy, in any case, was not phallic enough [or: not acephalic, *pas assez phalle*].

People mustn't count on me to structuralize life's impossibility [*l'affaire de la vie impossible*], as if it weren't precisely because of it that life has some chance of proving that it is real [or: that the real exists, *faire la preuve de son réel*].

My amusing prosopopoeia involving the "I speak" in the text I mentioned earlier, "The Freudian Thing," being rhetorically chalked up to a personified truth, does not make me fall from the place from whence I draw it [i.e., a well].

Nothing is said there other than what speaking means: the irremediable division between jouissance and semblance. Truth involves getting off on making believe [*faire semblant*], and never admitting that the reality of each of these two halves [jouissance and semblance] predominates solely by asserting that it depends on the other half – that is, by lying with the one half, and then with the other [*mentir à jets alternés*]. Such is the half-speaking of the truth.

Its astronomy is equatorial – in other words, already out of date – when it is born from the night/day pair.

An astronomy can only be reasoned out [*s'arraisonne*] by taking the seasons [*saisons*] into account, by being seasoned [*s'assaisonner*]. {This is an allusion to Chinese astronomy, which was equatorial and yielded nothing.}

It was not Freud's competence as a linguist, and for good reason, that allowed him to trace out the pathways of the thing in question. What I point out is that he could only follow these pathways by evincing linguistic performances, going so far as to perform high-wire acrobatics. Only linguistics allows us to situate those performances in a structure, insofar as it is linked to a competence that is known as linguistic consciousness, which is really quite remarkable in that it never eludes its inquiry.

152   Thus, my formulation that the unconscious is structured like a language indicates that the (pre)condition of the unconscious is, at a minimum, language.

But that in no wise lessens the import of the enigma that the unconscious knows more than it seems to, since it is owing to that surprise that it was called as it was called. It knows things. That immediately deteriorated, naturally, when all the instincts were attributed to it {those instincts are, moreover, still there, serving as a wet blanket. To convince yourself of this, it suffices to read anything that is published outside of my school}.

Things were all set; all they had to do was slap a label on it addressed to the truth, which has been overlooking it [or: which has been missing it, *laquelle la saute*] quite a lot in our times, as it were, so as not to disdain [or: not to forget, *pour ne pas dédaigner*] the black market.

I disrupted the rut of its clandestinity, by insisting that the knowledge in question could not be analyzed without being formulated like a language – namely, in a specific tongue, even if the latter had to be cross-pollinated, which is, moreover, no more than what the said tongues currently allow themselves to do without asking anyone for permission.

No one questioned me regarding what language knows – namely, *die Bedeutung des Phallus*. I had said it, of course, but no one noticed because it was the truth.

Who, then, is interested in truth? People. People whose structure I drew with the crude image of the Klein bottle, which you find in books on topology for the general public.

153   That's how you draw it [see Figure 9.2]. Let me repeat that there is not a single point of its surface that does not topologically participate in the looping back on itself [*rebroussement*] that is pictured here by the only circle that can give this bottle the ass [or: bottom, *cul*] that other bottles are unduly proud of, because in French they are said to have an ass, God only knows why.

Thus it is not where people think it is, but, rather, in her structure as a subject, that the hysteric – I am coming here to some of the people that I just mentioned – conjugates the truth of her jouissance with the implacable knowledge she has that the Other who is capable of causing that jouissance is the phallus – to wit, a semblance.

Who wouldn't understand Freud's disappointment when he realized that the lack of cure [or: cure-step, *pas-de-cure*] he arrived at with hysterics went no further than making them demand the said

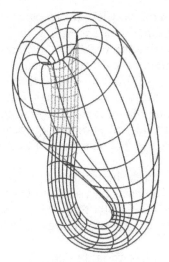

Figure 9.2 Klein Bottle

semblance (suddenly endowed with real virtues) from him, it having been encountered at the point of looping back on itself, which – not being unlocatable in the body, that is obvious – is a figuration that is altogether topologically incorrect of jouissance in a woman. But did Freud know it? {We can certainly wonder about that.}

In the impossible solution to her problem, it is by measuring its cause very carefully [*cause au plus juste*] – namely, by making it into a just cause [*juste cause*] – that the hysteric grants herself – among those she pretends possess this semblance – at least one (which I write, should I need to write it again, *hommoinzin*) who matches the bone(r) [or: is in keeping with the bone (or problem), *conforme à l'os*] necessary for her jouissance so that she can gnaw at it.

There are three different ways to write *hommoinzin*. There is, first of all, the usual spelling [*au moins un*], since, after all, I must explain it to you. Secondly, there is the expressive value that I always know how to give to scriptural play. Thirdly, we can write it – why wouldn't we? – *a(u moins un)*, so as not to forget that it can, at times, function as object *a*.

Since the *hommoinzin* cannot be broached by her without admitting to her target – who takes it however he likes – the deliberate castration she reserves for him, her chances are limited. We mustn't believe that her success [or: appeal] involves some one of these men, a masculine man, who is rather disconcerted by semblance, or who prefers it to be more obvious [*franc*]. The men I am designating in this way are sages, masochists. That situates sages. We have to put them in their proper place.

To assess the result in this way is to misrecognize what we can expect from the hysteric, assuming she is willing to be inscribed in a dis course. For she is destined to checkmate the master so that, thanks to her, he turn his attention back to knowledge.

{There you have it. All I am proposing here – the interest of this writing is that it generates a ton of things, but you have to know what is worth retaining – is that} the danger at this crossroads is the same as the one I just labeled about being warned, which is where I started out from earlier. {I come back to the same place, don't I? I go around in circles.}

To love the truth – even the truth that the hysteric incarnates, as it were – that is, to give her what you don't have on the pretext that she desires it, is very specifically to doom yourself to theatrics [or: theater] which can no longer be anything but a charity event – that's clear.

{I'm not speaking solely about hysterics. I'm talking about something that is expressed in the discontent, to say it like Freud does, in theater. For it to still hold up, we need Brecht, don't we, for he understood that this could not hold up without a certain distance, a certain cooling off.}

"That's clear," as I just said of "theatrics which can no longer be ...," is itself the effect of a barely believable *Aufklärung*: the arrival on the stage, however clumsily it happened, of the analyst's discourse. That sufficed for the hysteric {– the qualified hysteric whose function I am in the process, as you can sense, of broaching for you –} to discard the abundant symptoms with which she filled the gap in the relationship between the sexes.

We must perhaps take this as a sign, made to someone, that she is going to improve on that clinical picture.

The only thing that is important here is what goes unnoticed – namely, that I speak about hysterics as though they were susceptible of quantification.

Something would seem to be inscribed, if you listen to me, on the basis of an upside down A of x, $\forall x$, which is always able, with its unknown, to function as a variable in *Phi* of x, Φx.

That is, in fact, what I write, regarding which it would be easy, were we to reread Aristotle, to detect what relationship to woman, identified by him with the hysteric {which places the women of his time in a very good position, at the very least they were stimulating to men}, allowed him to establish his logic (and this involved a jump) through the choice of the word *pan, panta* {rather than that of *ekatos* [each] to designate the universal affirmative proposition, as well as the negative. In short, this whole *pan*-foolery [*pan-*

talonnade, means tomfoolery but also includes Aristotle's *pan*] of the first grand, formal logic is essentially linked to Aristotle's view of women.

The fact remains that the only universal formulation that he would not have allowed himself to pronounce is that involving "all women." There is no trace of that anywhere. Open his *Prior Analytics*. Although his successors went straight for it, he would not have allowed himself to write the incredibly stupid statement on which formal logic has relied ever since, "all men are mortal." That seals the fate of humanity. "All men are mortal" means that all men, since what is at stake here is something whose members are exhaustively enumerated [*en extension*], all men qua all [*tous les hommes en tant que tous*], are doomed to die – in other words, humankind is destined to disappear, which is at the very least rather brazen.}

The fact that V*x* requires us to shift to a being, an "all woman" [or: every woman, *toute femme*] that a being as sensitive as Aristotle never, in fact, committed to paper, is precisely what allows us to propose that "all woman" [or: every woman] is the enunciation by which the hysteric qua subject is determined [or: makes up her mind, *se décide*]. And this is why a woman is part and parcel of [*solidaire de*] a *papludun*, which strictly situates her in the logic of the successor that Peano provided for us as a model [the "successor function" or "successor operation"].

The hysteric is not *a* woman. It is important to know whether psychoanalysis, as I define it, provides access to *a* woman, or whether, if *a* woman comes into being, it is owing to *doxa*, like virtue was according to the people who dialogue with each other in Plato's *Meno* – do you recall the *Meno*? *Mais* no! The crux or meaning of that dialogue is that virtue is something that cannot be taught.

We can translate that by saying: what cannot be known in the unconscious, that is, in an articulated way, about her, about a woman, {such as I define the negation [or: step, *pas*].

I will pause here. In a very fine book, the author blathers on about theater as if it were a topic that should encompass a large swath of an analyst's activity, as if it were something that an analyst should truly study in depth. The author credits me in a footnote with having introduced the distinction between truth and knowledge. Preposterous!

I just mentioned the *Meno*, didn't I? Naturally, the aforementioned author never read it; he only reads plays. But it is thanks to the *Meno* that I began to go beyond the first phases of the crisis that pitted me against a certain psychoanalytic system. The distinction between truth and knowledge – i.e., between *episteme* and true *doxa* 156 [opinion], the latter being what can ground virtue – is laid out quite explicitly in the *Meno*. What I highlighted is the exact opposite: their junction – namely, that where they seem to come together to form a circle, the knowledge at stake in the unconscious is a kind of knowledge that slides [or: slips, *glisse*], persists, and turns out at every moment to be knowledge about truth.

It is here that I raise a question: does this knowledge effectively allow us to go beyond the *Meno*? Can this truth, insofar as it is incarnated in hysterics, slide flexibly enough to introduce us to *a* woman?}

I realize that the question has been taken up a notch since I demonstrated that there are things that can be linguistically articulated which are nevertheless not articulatable in words, and that that is the very thing that allows desire to be established.

Still, it is easy to answer the question. It is precisely because we are talking about desire, insofar as it stresses the invariance in the unknown {– which is on the left [∇x], the one that is produced only under the heading of a *Verneinung* [negation] –} that the carving out [*l'évidement*] of desire by analysis cannot inscribe it in any function with a variable [*function de variable*]. {That is the stumbling block [*butée*] owing to which the hysteric's desire actually separates from what is produced, and} allows innumerable women to function as such – in other words, by serving as *papludun* with their being for all sorts of situational variations.

{The hysteric plays the role there of a block diagram, if you know what that is.} This is the import of my formulation regarding what is known as "unsatisfied desire."

We can deduce from this that the hysteric situates herself by introducing the *papludun* on the basis of which *each* of the *women* is established, by the pathway of "it is not regarding every woman that it can be said that she is a function of the phallus" [$\overline{\nabla x}.\Phi x$]. The fact that it concerns every woman [or: all woman, *toute femme*] is what constitutes her desire, and this is why her desire is sustained by being unsatisfied – it is because *a* woman results therefrom, yet she cannot be the hysteric in person. It is in this regard that she incarnates the truth I mentioned earlier, the one that, after having made it speak, I returned to its structuralist function.

Analytic discourse is established by giving the hysteric back her truth. This sufficed to dissipate the theatrics in hysteria. This is why I say that it is not unrelated to something that changes the face of things in our era.

157   I stressed the fact that, when I first began to make statements that already hinted at all of these things, I immediately received a

reaction in an article (which made quite a "splash"*) about theatrics in hysterics. Contemporary psychoanalysis resorts only to hysterics who are not up-to-date [*à la page*]. When the latter prove that, having turned the page, they continue to write on the other side of it, and even on the next page, analysts don't understand. For hysterics are logicians.

This raises the question why Freudian theory refers to theater – Oedipus, no less.

It is high time to broach the facet of theater that it seemed necessary to maintain in order to undergird the Other scene {the scene I was the first to talk about}. Sleep perhaps suffices to get us into it, after all. And the fact that it may, at times, harbor the embryo of Fuchsian functions, as you know happened, can justify that a desire to go on sleeping arises.

The signifying representatives of the subject may do ever more easily without being borrowed from imaginary representation. {We see signs of this in our era.}

It is clear that the jouissance of which we must get ourselves castrated has only system-like relations [*rapports d'appareil*] with representation.

It is in this respect that Sophocles' *Oedipus* – which we privilege simply because the other Oedipus stories are either incomplete or lost – is still far too rich and diffuse for our purposes.

The genealogy of desire – insofar as what we want to know is how it is caused [or: is spoken, *se cause*] – is connected to a more complex combinatory than that of the myth of Oedipus.

This is why we need not dream about what purpose the myth served "back in the day," as they say. To go down that path is to employ metalanguage, and the mythologies of Lévi-Strauss have made a decisive contribution on this topic. They show that the combining of countable forms of a mytheme, many of which have disappeared, occurs according to precise transformational laws; yet that combination follows a rather meager logic, or at least a logic about which we must say – it's the least we can say – that our mathematics enriches that combinatory.

We should perhaps wonder whether psychoanalysts don't have better things to do than spend their time interpreting such myths, for they go no deeper than other typical commentaries – which are, moreover, completely superfluous, because what the ethnologist is interested in is collecting, collating, and recollating the myth with other functions, whether those related to ritual or production, enumerated similarly in a writing whose articulated isomorphisms suit it.

We find no trace here of a supposition, I was going to say, regarding the jouissance that is isolated therein. This is quite true, even if we take into account the efforts made to suggest to us that obscure knowledge systems might possibly be operating behind them. The note provided by Lévi-Strauss, in his *Elementary Structures of Kinship*, about the action of display that is exercised by structures in the realm of love is, fortunately, decisive here.

It, nevertheless, went right over the heads of the psychoanalysts who were in favor at the time.

In short, Oedipus has the advantage of showing in what respect man can (cor)respond to the need in a woman's being for the *papludun*. He himself would love *papludune* [no more than one (woman)]. Unfortunately, it is not the same one. It is always the same appointment with fate, when the masks fall: it was neither him nor her.

Yet this fable is underpinned solely by the fact that man is never anything but a little boy. The fact that the hysteric can't let go of that casts doubt on the function of the last word of her truth.

A step toward seriousness could, it seems to me, help us get a handle on man whom, you will note, I have thus far given but a modest place in my exposé– even if yours truly is himself one of this fine set of people.

It strikes me as impossible – and it is no accident that I run up against this word right from the outset – not to grasp the divide that separates the Oedipus myth from the myth of the father of the primal horde found in *Totem and Taboo*.

I will show my cards right away. The first myth is dictated to Freud by the hysteric's lack of satisfaction, the second by his own impasses.

There is no trace in the second myth of what makes up the first myth: a little boy, his mother, and the tragedy involved in the passage from the father to the son – of what, if not the phallus?

In *Totem and Taboo*, the father enjoys, a term that is veiled in the first myth by power [or: potency, *puissance*]. The father enjoys all the women until his sons kill him, having made an agreement before doing so, after which none of them succeed him in his sexual gluttony. A term forces itself upon us owing to what happens by way of an aftershock: the sons devour him, each one necessarily receiving only one morsel, which thus turns it into a communion.

It is on this basis that the social contract comes into being: no one shall touch, not the mother – it is clearly indicated in *Moses and Monotheism*, which flowed from Freud's own pen, that only the youngest sons are still allowed in the harem. It is the father's wives who are targeted by the prohibition. {The mother plays a role only with her babies, who are made of the stuff of heroes.

Yet if this is, according to Freud,} how the law originates, it does not originate from the so-called law against incest with the mother, which is, nevertheless, taken to be inaugural in psychoanalysis; for, in fact – aside from a certain law of Manu that punishes it with real castration {("You shall proceed to the west with your balls in your hand . . .")} – the law against maternal incest is, instead, elided everywhere.

I am certainly not contesting the prophylactic well-foundedness of the analytic prohibition, but I am highlighting the fact that Freud does not mythically justify it when he articulates something in *Totem and Taboo*, and Lord knows it was dear to him. The strange thing is that Freud does not seem to have noticed this; nor has anyone else, for that matter.

I will continue in the same vein. Jouissance is raised by Freud to the rank of an absolute, which brings us back to the good offices of the earliest man – and all of that is avowed – the Father of the primal horde. It is easy as pie to recognize the phallus there: it is the totality of what can femininely be subject to jouissance. As I just commented, this jouissance remains veiled in the royal couple in *Oedipus*, but it is not totally absent in that myth.

The royal couple is called into question only on the basis of the fact, which is stated in the tragedy, that they are the guarantors of the people's jouissance, which, moreover, concords with what we know about all royalties, both ancient and modern.

Oedipus's castration has no other goal than to bring the Theban plague to an end – in other words, to restore jouissance to the people, jouissance of which others will now be the guarantors – and, given where we began, this obviously won't happen without a few bitter incidents for one and all.

Must I highlight the fact that, in the two myths, the key functions are diametrically opposed? In the first, the law comes first, and it is so primordial that it punishes even when guilty parties have only transgressed innocently; the profusion of jouissance stems from the law.

In the second myth, we find jouissance at the outset and law later; you will spare me the trouble of highlighting how this correlates with perversion, since, in the final analysis – in addition to promoting secret cannibalism, which people emphasize considerably – it is *all the women* who are prohibited, on principle, to the community of males, which transcends itself through this communion. That is clearly the meaning of the other primordial law, without which what could establish it? I believe that Eteocles and Polynices, the sons of Oedipus who killed each other, prove that there are other resources. It is true that they proceed from the genealogy of desire.

Was the killing of the father so incredibly fascinating – to whom? to Freud? to his readers? – that no one even dreamt of emphasizing that, in the first myth, the murder occurs unbeknownst to the murderer? Oedipus not only does not recognize that he is striking his father, but cannot recognize his father because he has another father – a man who has served as his father since the outset, having adopted Oedipus as an infant. Indeed, it was so as not to run the risk of striking this latter father that he deliberately went into exile. The myth is suggestive: it manifests the place the biological father had at a time at which the father was problematic, as Freud stresses, just as he is in our times.

For Oedipus would have been absolved were he not of royal blood – in other words, if Oedipus didn't have to function as the phallus, his people's phallus, not his mother's. The most surprising thing is that it worked for a while – the Thebans were very happy. I have often indicated that the change in direction had to come from Jocasta. Is it owing to the fact that she knew or the fact that she didn't know [or: ignored it, *ignoré*]?

What could this possibly have in common, in any case, with the murder found in the second myth, which seems to have resulted from a revolt, from need? Which is truly unthinkable – nay, unthought – unless it proceeded from a conspiracy.

It is clear that all I have done here is broach a topic which, let us say, a conspiracy stopped *me* from truly broaching {– in other words, *Moses and Monotheism*, namely, the point in relation to which everything Freud articulated becomes truly significant}. 161 I can't even begin to sketch out what it would take to pinpoint Freud's contribution to analytic discourse there; but I can say that, in revealing it, he proceeds no less on the basis of neurosis than regarding what he learned from hysterics in the form of Oedipus.

It is curious that it has taken me this long to be able to propose such an assertion – namely, that *Totem and Taboo* is a neurotic product, a claim that is altogether indisputable – without having to call into question the truth of the construction in any way whatsoever. Which goes to show that it attests to the truth. You don't psychoanalyze a text by anyone, and still less one by Freud. You criticize it, and rather than rendering its solidity suspect, neurosis in fact solidifies it in this case.

We owe Freud's myth to the structure of the relationship between the sexes – attested to by the obsessive – that is impossible to formulate in discourse.

I will stop there today. Next time, I will give that its precise import, for I wouldn't like there to be any misunderstanding.

To articulate Freud's contribution to the fundamental myth of psychoanalysis in a way that highlights its origin, is in no wise to render it suspect – quite the contrary.

We simply need to know where that can take us.

June 9, 1971

X

ON THE MYTH FREUD MADE

There's no such thing as a sexual relationship
Between jouissance and semblance
There is only one *Bedeutung*
To speak in the Name-of-the-Father
Freud and the *papludun*

Today I am going to try to establish the meaning of the road by which I have led you this year with the title "On a discourse that might not be a semblance" [or "On a discourse that would (like) not (to) be about semblance"].

I presented this title to you in the conditional tense, for it is an hypothesis, the one on the basis of which all discourse is justified.

Don't forget that last year I tried to divide up the discourses you deal with into four typical discourses. I broke them down into four, believing that I justified this in the discussion of them I provided in a writing entitled "*Radiophonie*" – paradoxically, but not all that paradoxically if you heard [or: understood] what I said last time. These discourses are laid out in a certain order, which is, of course, justified only on the basis of history. That writing reminds you of the four terms in these discourses, of their ever syncopated slippage [or: rotation], and of the fact that there is always a gap between two of them.

These discourses – which I designated as the master's discourse, the university discourse, the hysteric's discourse, as I dubbed it, and the analyst's discourse – have a certain property, which is to always be organized around semblance. That organizing principle is also the one that gives each discourse its name.

What makes analytic discourse special, such that it is the one that allows us to articulate all four, and to divide them up into four fundamental arrays?

It is odd that such an enunciation presents itself as if at the endpoint of what Freud – he who happened to be at the origin of analytic discourse – allowed.

164   He didn't allow it on the basis of nothing. He allowed it on the basis of what presents itself – I have often articulated this – as the core of the analyst's discourse, namely, what gets prioritized owing to a certain knowledge that sheds light on the relationship between truth and knowledge.

1

It is strictly speaking prodigious that it was from neurotics, namely hysterics and obsessives – the very people who seem to be crippled (or, to be kinder, who seem lame, and it is well known that beauty limps) when seen from a certain angle, a societal angle – that emanated the light that flashed across the whole of the *demansion* conditioned by language; in other words, the function that truth is, or even, at times, the crystallization whose role in Freud's work everyone is aware of, and which is what we know of as religion in its modern form – namely, the Judeo-Christian tradition, on which everything Freud said about religion bears.

Let me remind you that this is consistent with the subverting of what was maintained up until then through the entire knowledge tradition, as we might call it. This subverting operation originated with the notion of the symptom.

It is important to realize that, historically speaking, the originality of psychoanalysis, as created by Freud, does not lie there. I have indicated several times that the notion of the symptom was introduced by Marx, and it is very easy to locate in his work.

The dimension of semblance was introduced by the fundamental dupery exposed by Marx's subversion of the theory of knowledge, in a certain tradition that arrived at its culmination with Hegel; correlatively, some semblance was established in the role of weights and measures [or: double standards, *de poids et mesure*], as it were, which were taken at face value [literally, taken as though they were cold cash, *argent comptant*]. It is no accident that I am employing these specific metaphors, since it is regarding money and capital as such that we see the pivotal point in his exposé indicating that the thing

165   that must be put back in its place – through a reversal of thought, insofar as it is quite precisely semblance – lies in the fetish.

The singular nature of this remark is designed to make us perceive the following. In exposing this, something was stated that was posited as truth. In the name of this truth, surplus value emerged as the mainspring of that which had been propped up until then by a certain number of deliberate misrecognitions, and which had to be reduced to its semblance. But this irruption of truth was insufficient – as I pointed out and as history demonstrates – to destroy what was propped up by the discourse that was thus exposed.

Instead, this discourse – which we might, in this case, call capitalist discourse insofar as it stems from the master's discourse – found therein its complement. Far from it being the case that capitalism suffered from the recognition of the role played by surplus value, it appears to have done just fine, since what seems to have resulted, in the form of a political revolution, from Marx's exposé of a certain discourse based on semblance, is a form of capitalism taken up in a master's discourse.

This is why I will not dwell here on the historic mission that was reserved for the proletariat in Marxism, at least in its manifestoes. We see there, I would say, a remainder of humanist entification which, turning the proletariat into those who are the most impoverished in capitalism, nevertheless demonstrates that something persists that makes them remain impoverished. The fact that they prop up what is produced by way of surplus value in no way frees them from articulating it.

Which is why this exposé leads us to investigate something that might take us back further in time, and that might turn out to be at the very origin of every discourse insofar as it is based on semblance. Thus, what I articulated with the term "surplus jouissance" brings us to what Freud investigated by calling into question the relationship between semblance and something that is articulated as truth. If what Freud said has any meaning, the dialectic of truth and semblance is situated at the level of what I designated with the term "sexual relationship" [or: "relationship between the sexes," *rapport sexuel*].

In short, I dared to incite people to realize that what the neurotic's knowledge reveals to us is no other than the following: there's no such thing as a sexual relationship. 166

What does that mean? It can be said, since it *has* now been said, but naturally it does not suffice to say it – it must be explained. Our explanations stem from our experience, from the thread of what is tied to this fundamental gap. There lies its central point of departure. The thread we follow gets wrapped around the void [*vide*] in what I call the neurotic's discourse.

Last time, I clearly highlighted where this thread begins, attempting to broach it with something I wrote. My intention today is to situate, not what the neurotic indicates, owing to his relationship to this distance – the thing goes beyond or lies at the extreme edge

of what can be said in the limited space of a Seminar – but what is
indicated by the myths on the basis of which the myth Freud forged
was constructed, not as dictated by the neurotic's discourse in every
instance, but echoing it nevertheless.

In order to do so in such a short space of time, we must begin
with this central, yet enigmatic, point in psychoanalytic discourse,
insofar as it pays attention solely to this last discourse here [i.e., the
neurotic's discourse], the one that might not be a semblance [or: that
would (like) not (to) be based on semblance]. It listens to a discourse
that would (like) not (to) be, and that, moreover, is not [based on
(or: about) semblance]. I mean that what is indicated here is merely
the limit imposed on discourse when what is at issue is the relationship between the sexes. Given where I am at, where I am trying to
make headway, where every bit of progress is sketched out, I myself
have tried to tell you that this has to do with its failure at the level
of a logic that is propped up by what props up any and every logic
– namely, writing.

The letter of Freud's work is a written work. But what it sketches
out with these writings surrounds a veiled, obscure truth, a truth that
can be stated as follows: a relationship between the sexes, such as it
occurs in any sexual act, is based only on the compromise between
[or: combining of, *composition entre*] jouissance and semblance that is
known as castration. We see it re-emerge constantly in the neurotic's
discourse, but in the form of fear and avoidance, and it is precisely in
that sense that castration remains enigmatic. However shifting and
shimmering the concrete forms castration takes – or, what's more,
the exploration of the psychopathology of analyzable phenomena
that allow for excursions into ethnology – the fact remains that what
distinguishes everything that falls under the heading of castration
takes what form? The form of avoidance. In every case.

167

If the neurotic attests to the necessary intrusion, as it were, of
what I just called a compromise between [or: combining of] jouissance and semblance that presents itself as castration, it is precisely
insofar as he shows himself to be in some way unfit.

You know about initiation rites – if you don't, have a look at
the specialized works on the subject. To take just two that were
produced within the analytic field itself, I will mention *Problems of
Bisexuality as Reflected in Circumcision* by Herman Nunberg, which
came out in Englewood, New Jersey (which is actually Imago in
London [1949]), and secondly, the book entitled *Symbolic Wounds:
Puberty Rites and the Envious Male* by Bruno Bettelheim [New
York: Collier, 1962]. In them you will see, deployed in all its ambiguity and fundamental wavering, how analytic thought hesitates
between (1) an explanatory system at the core of which lies an

opaque fear of castration, and (2) the enumeration of accidents by which, depending on one's luck or lack thereof, castration presents itself – which, in this register, would merely be the effect of some sort of misunderstanding. In this thicket of biases and blunders, castration is something rectifiable, on the one hand, and yet people realize that there is truly some constancy there, on the other hand.

At the very least, a huge number of works we can find in all fields – even if the catalogs aren't always well constructed, whether those produced in ethnology or psychopathology, which I mentioned earlier, and there are still others – force us to face the fact that there is no such thing as a sexual relationship.

Freud sometimes said as much. He said it very well in *Civilization and Its Discontents*, making what I formulate not so new after all. Freud indicated, as I did, in terms that are altogether clear, that fate undoubtedly intervenes in relations between the sexes, making necessary what then appear to be the means, bridges, connecting paths, edifices, and, in short, constructions that (cor)respond to the missing relationship between the sexes. The result is that, in a sort of reversal of perspective, every possible discourse can appear as nothing other than the symptom that, within the relationship between the sexes – and under conditions, that, as usual, we cast back into prehistory, into extra-historical realms – makes something succeed, to some degree. The symptom makes something artificial – something that might be established, supplementing what is lacking, and that is inscribed in speaking beings – succeed. But this doesn't tell us whether it is because they speak that this is the way it is, or if, on the contrary, it is because the relationship is not speakable that something must develop, for all those who inhabit language, that renders possible – in the guise of castration – the gap left open in what is nevertheless biologically essential to the reproduction of these beings as living beings, so that their race remains fruitful.

Indeed, this is the problem that all initiation rites seem to try to grapple with. These rights include what we will call manipulations, operations, incisions, and circumcisions that target, and put their mark on, the very organ that we see function as a symbol in analytic experience, going well beyond the privilege of the organ, since it is the phallus. It is around this third-party [the phallus] that everything that blocks [or: serves as an obstacle to] jouissance revolves, making men and women – insofar as we define them with simple biological labels – into beings who have difficulty with sexual jouissance, more so than with all the other jouissances.

This is clearly what is at issue, and it is from here that we must start out anew if we want analytic discourse to continue in the right direction.

We assume that it is something defined, which we call castration, that has the special ability to deal with something whose undecidability constitutes the crux of the relationship between the sexes, inasmuch as it gives us jouissance as organized with regard to the following statements that strike me as unavoidable.

The dramaturgy of constraint, which is the everyday fare of analytic discourse, runs altogether counter to the only thing that is important, which is not to locate initiation rites in prehistory, like everything else we might want to cast back into prehistory. This remark is particularly relevant to the second book that I mentioned, the one by Bruno Bettelheim. These rites still exist and are found the world over. There are still Australians who undergo circumcision and incision. There are whole civilizations that subject themselves to such things. We must not overlook the fact that these practices not only persist in a century of supposed enlightenment, but are alive and well, being widespread. We must obviously take that into account if we are to perceive that these rites stem from no conceivable dramaturgy of constraint whatsoever. None of the examples show that it is constraint alone that is at work.

We must, moreover, clarify what constraint means. Constraint – the supposed presence of physical or other superiority – is based on signifiers. If it is a law or rule that makes it such that one or another subject is willing to submit himself to that rite, it is truly for reasons, and these reasons are what are of concern to us.

What is of concern to us is the subject's willingness [*complaisance*] – to employ a term which, although it takes us straight to hysterics, is nevertheless of extremely wide scope – that allows what presents itself as something whose image would, in and of itself, be unbearable, to subsist in times that are altogether historical.

It is perhaps actually unbearable, and we need to know why.

That is where I will pick the thread up anew.

It is by following this thread that we can give meaning to what is articulated in psychoanalysis, in what I will call this unheralded speech – for it was unheralded up to a certain point in time, which was clearly historical and within our grasp – that presents itself as always having to remain unheralded, at least in part, since the unconscious can be defined in no other way.

Since I like beginning with hysterics, let us now turn to them to try to see where this thread takes us.

2

What are hysterics, we ask ourselves? What does the hysteric in person mean?

I believe that we have worked on the imaginary long enough that I can simply remind you of what is already inscribed in this term. "In person" means "masked." No immediate answer can be given here. To the question "What are hysterics?" the answer given by analytic discourse is "You shall see" if you follow where they lead. 170

Without hysterics, what I write as Φ of x – in trying to give you the first logical sketch of what is now at stake – would never have come to light. In other words, jouissance – the variable, x, inscribed in the function – can only be situated on the basis of its relationship with capital Φ, which designates the phallus here.

The phallus is a central discovery, or rather a rediscovery or renaming, as you like. I have told you why the term was taken up anew, and this was no accident, from the phallus qua semblance that was unveiled in the Mysteries. Indeed, all sexual jouissance that can be organized and contained hinges on the phallus as semblance. Freud leads us there, right from his very first attempt to broach hysteria in his *Studies on Hysteria*.

Last time I articulated the following: by taking things up from the point that can, in fact, be investigated, regarding the status of the most everyday discourse, if we wish to extrapolate from what linguistics tells us (without following linguistics all the way), we realize that none of what language allows us to do is ever anything but metaphor or metonymy. What any speech whatsoever claims to denote, if only for an instant, can never point to anything but a connotation.

As I said last time, if there is something that can, in the final analysis, be pointed to as being denoted by any linguistic function whatsoever, it is a *Bedeutung* – there is only one, *die Bedeutung des Phallus* [the Signification of the Phallus]. That is the only thing that is denoted by language, but nothing can ever answer when it is called upon. If there is something that characterizes the phallus, it is *not* that it is the signifier of lack – as some people believed they could understand certain of my words – but rather something from which no words flow.

As I also reminded you last time, we, especially we analysts, should keep many things in mind that are discussed in an article by Frege, a truly inaugural logician – above all, the two notions, *Sinn* and *Bedeutung*, for they give rise to models that go further than those involving connotation and denotation. Should we fail to study logic – and classical Aristotelian logic obviously cannot suffice for our purposes – it will be impossible to find the right vantage point [*point juste*] regarding the ideas that I am proposing.

171   Frege remarks that, having arrived at a certain point in scientific discourse, we can ask the following questions: Is it the same thing to say "Venus" as it is to employ the two terms by which it was long designated: "the evening star" and "the morning star"? Are we saying the same thing when we say "Sir Walter Scott" as when we say "the author of *Waverley*"? Let me inform those of you who might not be aware of this that Scott is, indeed, the author of the book entitled *Waverley*. It is by examining this distinction that Frege realizes that it is not possible in every case to replace "Sir Walter Scott" by "the author of *Waverley*." This is why he proposes that "the author of *Waverley*" conveys a meaning – that is, a *Sinn* – whereas "Sir Walter Scott" designates a *Bedeutung*.

According to Leibniz, we must posit – *salva veritate*, in order to "save the truth" – that any two terms that designate the same *Bedeutung* can be used interchangeably. Let us immediately put this to the test by using the example provided by Frege himself. It doesn't matter whether it was George the third, or George the fourth who tried to find out whether Sir Walter was the author of *Waverley*. If we replace "the author of *Waverley*" by "Sir Walter Scott," we obtain the following sentence: "King George III tried to find out if Sir Walter Scott was Sir Walter Scott," which obviously does not have the same meaning. Frege grounds his fundamental distinction between *Sinn* and *Bedeutung* on this simple logical remark.

It is clear that one *Bedeutung* always gestures toward another *Bedeutung* that is further off, and this is related to the distinction Frege makes between "oblique discourse" and "direct discourse." It is inasmuch as what George III asks is placed in an interrogative subordinate clause that we must give the *Sinne* their due here; we can, in no case, replace "the author of *Waverley*" by "Sir Walter Scott."

But that is, of course, an artifice, which leads us to the following point: Sir Walter Scott is, in this case, a name. And when Carnap returns to the question of *Bedeutung*, he translates it as "nominatum," whereby he slid in a direction he should not have slid. My comments can allow us to go further, but certainly not in the same direction as Carnap.

Last time, I said – and I will repeat it today – that we need to know what a name means. It is easy for us to connect this up here with what I indicated earlier. I pointed out that the phallus is what
172   brings us toward the point that I designate here by accentuating the difference between "name"* and "noun"* [Lacan uses English here as they are both the same in French: *nom*]. We see things clearly

solely at the level of the proper name [*nom propre*]. As the man said, a name is what calls on you. Undoubtedly, but to do what? It calls on you to speak. What is unique about the phallus is that you can call on it until the cows come home and it will never say anything.

And yet this gives meaning to what, back in the day, I called the "paternal metaphor," and that is where the hysteric leads us. When I introduced the paternal metaphor in my article "On a Question Prior to Any Possible Treatment of Psychosis," I inserted it in the general schema derived by relating what linguistics tells us about metaphor to what the experience of the unconscious teaches us about condensation. I wrote it S over S prime, multiplied by S prime over lowercase x, from which results $S(1/x)$ [*Écrits*, p. 464]. I clearly emphasized – for I also stated this in "The Instance of the Letter" [p. 428] – the fact that metaphors generate meaning. If "the author of *Waverley*" is a *Sinn*, it is precisely because "the author of *Waverley*" replaces something else, which is a special *Bedeutung*, the one that Frege believes he must designate with the name "Sir Walter Scott."

But this is not the only perspective from which I envisioned the paternal metaphor. I wrote somewhere that the Name-of-the-Father is the phallus – and Lord knows what a tremor of horror this evoked in certain pious souls – because at that time I could not articulate it any better. The Name-of-the-Father is, of course, the phallus, but it is still the Name-of-the-Father. If what is named Father, the Name-of-the-Father, is a name that has some efficacy, it is precisely because someone stands up to answer when it is pronounced. From the perspective of what occurred in Schreber's psychosis, I was able to correctly situate the Name-of-the-Father qua signifier capable of giving meaning to the mother's desire.

But when it is, let's say, the hysteric who calls upon the Name-of-the-Father, she expects someone to stand up and speak. Freud sometimes tried to examine more closely the function of the Father. The latter is so essential to analytic discourse that one can, in a certain way, say that it is its own product. If I write analytic discourse for you as follows –

$$\frac{a}{S_2}$$

173

– in other words, the analyst over the knowledge he has thanks to neurotics, and questioning the subject, S barred, in order to produce something that I note S_1 – it is because we can say that the master signifier in analytic discourse has, up until now, been the Name-of-the-Father.

It is extremely curious that, for questions to be raised about this, analytic discourse had to come into being. What is a father? Freud did not hesitate to articulate that it is the name which, by its very essence, brings in [or: implies, *implique*] the law. That is how he expressed himself. We might nevertheless want a bit more. After all, if we take things up solely at the biological level, we can perfectly well imagine the reproduction of the human species occurring without the Name-of-the-Father intervening in any way. This has already been conceptualized; it flowed from a novelist's imagination. It is no accident that there is such a thing as artificial insemination. What constitutes the presence, which is no recent invention, of the father's essence? Do we analysts clearly know what it is?

I would like, all the same, to point out that in analytic experience, the father is never anything but a frame of reference [*référentiel*]. We interpret some relation or another to the father. Do we ever analyze anyone *qua* father?

Show me a case study that does so. The father is a term in analytic interpretation. Things point to him.

3

I will have to merely sketch things out here. Still, I would like to situate the status of the Oedipal myth for you in light of these remarks.

The Oedipal myth is problematic because it supposedly establishes the primacy of the father, which is said to have some sort of patriarchal glint. I would like to convey to you in what respect it does not seem, at least to me, to have a patriarchal glint at all – far from it. It shows us the way in which castration can be isolated by approaching it logically, and in a way that I will designate as being number-based [or: numeral, *numérale*].

174   The father is not merely castrated, but castrated to the point of being no more than a number. We see this very clearly in dynasties. I spoke earlier about a king, and I wasn't sure if he was George III or George IV. This is what strikes me as most typical in the presentation of paternity. In reality, that's how it happens: George I, George II, George III, and George IV. But that does not exhaustively answer the question, because there is not only the numeral [or: digit, *le numéro*], there is a number [or: count, *un nombre*]. In short, I see there the point of apperception of the series of natural numbers, as it is put. It is put not too badly, for after all, it is very close to nature.

Since people always gesture toward history, which is a good reason to be extremely suspicious of it, I would simply like to point out that matriarchy, as it is put, has no need to be located at the very limit between prehistory and history.

Matriarchy consists essentially in the following: there is no doubt who one's mother is. One can, at times, lose one's mother in the subway, of course, but there is no doubt as to who she is. Nor is there any doubt regarding who her mother was. And so on and so forth. In their lineage, mothers are uncountable [or: innumerable, *innombrable*], I would say. They are uncountable in all the strict senses of the term: they cannot be counted, for there is no starting point. The maternal line necessarily proceeds in a certain order, but we cannot consider it to begin anywhere in particular.

I could also point out, on the other hand, the fact – and this is something we seem to come across all the time, because it is not at all rare – that one's father can be one's grandfather. I mean that one's grandfather – and even one's great grandfather – can be one's biological father. We are told that, in the first line of the patriarchs, people lived about 900 years. I read that again recently and it's very striking – it's an absolutely sensational fabrication. Things are concocted in such a way that the two most direct ancestors of Noah are dead just when the flood occurs. We see that it is carefully crafted. Well, let us set that aside. I'm saying it just to give you a sense of the status of fathers.

I am obliged to move along at a good clip here because it is getting late. If we define neurosis as the avoidance of castration, let us note that there are several different ways to avoid it. The hysteric does it quite simply: she attributes it to her partner. What the hysteric needs is a castrated partner. 175

Her jouissance depends upon his castration. But that is still too much. Were he castrated, he might still have a chance. For, as I said earlier, castration is what allows for the relationship between the sexes. The partner must be no more than what responds in the stead of the phallus.

Freud himself tells us something (I am not going to give you the page number) about the historical hypothesis he developed, the one by Sellin that he revamped, in the form of a myth involving Moses, which he published in 1938. The French translation reads as follows: "I won't critique it here, for all the results we have arrived at constitute psychological deductions that stem from it, and constantly refer back to it." As you can see, that doesn't mean squat. In German, it means something: *denn sie bilden die Voraussetzung*, "for they form the supposition," *der psychologischen Erörterungen*, "of psychological manifestations, which, based on these data," *die von ihnen ausgehen*, "stem and are ever further," *auf sie zurückkommen*, "corroborated." Indeed, it is clearly as dictated by the hysteric – not that Oedipus was developed, for he was never truly developed by Freud – that Oedipus was pointed out on the horizon, in the smoke, as it were, of what rises up in the guise of the hysteric's sacrifice. But let us now clearly observe what this naming, this response to calling on the father, means in the Oedipal myth.

I mentioned earlier that this introduces the series of natural numbers, because we have here something that turned out to be necessary in the most recent logical elaboration of this series, the one by Peano: not the simple fact of succession, but the necessity of zero to establish the successor. I will not dwell here on the commentaries that perfected this. When we try to axiomatize the possibility of such a series, we realize that the last of Peano's minimal axioms is the one that posits zero as necessary to this series, without which it can in no wise be axiomatized, without which it would be uncountable, as I said earlier.

The logical function I employed is too often forgotten. I can provide you with its equivalent only marginally and very quickly. 176 Let me point out that in the year 2000 we will, to the best of my knowledge, be entering into the second millennium. If you simply accept that – on the other hand, you may not – I will point out that it implies that there was a year zero after Christ's birth. That is something that the authors of the Republican calendar in France forgot, for they called the first year of the Republic year I.

Zero is absolutely essential to any natural chronological situating. We can thus understand what is meant by the killing of the father.

Isn't it curious and odd that the killing of the father never appears, even in tragedies, as is pointed out relevantly by someone who wrote a halfway decent chapter on the subject. No tragedian has ever dared, says that author, to stage the deliberate killing by a son of his father qua father. Pay close attention to that. It never occurs even in Ancient Greek theater. Yet the killing of the father appears at the center of what Freud proposes on the basis of data that constitute, owing to the hysteric, the refusal of castration.

Isn't it insofar as the killing of the father takes the place of this refused castration, that Oedipus forced himself on Freud's thinking as he broached the topic of hysteria? It is clear that, from the hysteric's perspective, it is the phallus that fertilizes, and what it begets is itself, as it were. Fecundity is phallic forgery, and it is in this sense that every child reproduces the phallus insofar as it is replete [or: pregnant, *gros*], if I may put it thus, with its begetting.

Yet, since it is on the basis of the *papludun* [no-more-than-one] that I designated the logicized possibility of choice in the unsatisfied relation of the relationship between the sexes, we also glimpse from whence derives Freud's unbelievable indulgence regarding a monotheism whose model he seeks – and this is very curious – elsewhere than in his own tradition. For him it has to be Akhenaton. Nothing is more ambiguous, sexually speaking, than this solar monotheism, when we see it shine with all its rays, rays that are provided with little hands that tickle the nostrils of countless little humans, children of one sex and the other. It is striking, in this imagery of Oedipal structure, that they resemble each other like brothers – that's the word for it – and even more like sisters. If the word "sublime" can be ambiguous, it is clearly there. And it is no accident that the last monumental images of Akhenaton that I was able to see the last time I was in Egypt are not merely castrated, but clearly feminine.

If castration is related to the phallus, Φ of x, it is certainly not there that we can designate it. Indeed, the little schema, in which the "not all (men)" or "not all (women)" [*pas tous* ou *pas toutes*] designates a certain type of relation to Φ of x, clearly means that the exceptions [or: chosen (or elect), *élus*] *are* related to Φ of x. 177

The shift to mediation, in quotes, is merely the mediation of this "at least one" that I highlighted, and that we find anew in Peano's work in the $n + 1$ which is forever repeated, the one that assumes in some sense that the n that precedes it is reduced to zero. How is it reduced to zero? By killing the Father. The meaning of the killing of the Father is related to a *Bedeutung*, that of the phallus, by this situating or detour – or oblique path, *ungerade*, to employ the term Frege himself uses.

I will have to stop there today. I apologize for not having been able to take things further. That will have to wait until next year. I am sorry that things were necessarily truncated this year.

On the other hand, an avoidance that is strictly equivalent to castration corresponds to what, in *Totem and Taboo*, situates the earliest jouissance in the father. This clearly indicates how the obsessive – in response to the formula that there exists no x that can be inscribed in the variable Φ of x [$\overline{\exists x.\Phi x}$] – slips away. He does so simply by not existing. That is where I will pick up anew – why not? – the thread of my discourse next year.

The obsessive personifies debt [*est dans la dette*] because he does not exist with regard to the no-less-mythical Father, the one who is discussed in *Totem and Taboo*. Everything regarding a certain religious edification truly connects up with that, as well as with the respect in which it is, alas, not eliminable, not even from what Freud links to his second myth, the one in *Totem and Taboo* – namely, no more nor less than his second topography. We will be able to discuss this at a later date. Note that the big innovation in the second topography is the superego.

What is the essence of the superego? It is on this point that I will end today by giving you something you can hold in the palm of your hand, and that you can try to work with yourselves. How is the superego organized? It finds its origin in the Father, who is more primal than mythical, in the call for pure jouissance – in other words, for noncastration. Indeed, what does this Father say at the moment of the dissolution of the Oedipus complex? He says what the superego says. It is no accident that I have never really broached this. What the superego says is "Enjoy!"

That is the order – which is impossible to follow – that is at the origin of everything that develops under the heading of moral conscience, regardless of how paradoxical this may seem to you. To get a real feel for its scope [*jeu*], and even its derision, you must read the following words in *Ecclesiastes* [9:9]: "Enjoy such as you are, enjoy," as the author (who is enigmatic, as you know) of this astonishing text says, "Enjoy life with the woman you love."

This is the height of the paradox, because the obstacle arises precisely from loving her.

June 16, 1971

Appendix

A NUMBER OF REFERENCES THAT LACAN MAKES TO HIS OWN WORK, AND TO THAT OF OTHERS

by Jacques-Alain Miller

Class I. Lacan immediately refers to three moments of his teaching: *The Other Side of Psychoanalysis*, his Seminar from the year before, the first class of which lays out the theory of the four discourses; issue number 2/3 of his journal *Scilicet* which includes his article entitled "Radiophonie," which ends with the schema of those same discourses (the article is included in the collection entitled *Autres Écrits*); and "Function and Field of Speech and Language in Psychoanalysis," his "Rome Report" or "Rome Discourse" (the inaugural 1953 text that is included in the collection entitled *Écrits*). The person who "contributed to the deciphering of *Verneinung*" was the philosopher Jean Hippolyte (see Seminar I and *Écrits*; his text is included in [an appendix of] the latter).

Class II. *Che vuoi?*: a question asked in *The Devil in Love* by Jacques Cazotte, which Lacan took up as the question of the Other's desire in "Subversion of the Subject and Dialectic of Desire in the Freudian Unconscious" (in *Écrits*). Bishop Berkeley's idealism is commented on specifically in Seminar XVI. Plato and Aristotle: Lacan refers to them regularly. "I am not a nominalist": see, in the same vein, *Autres Écrits*, pp. 327–28. Lacan comments on the schema found in Freud's *Massenpsychologie* [*Group Psychology and the Analysis of the Ego*] (Chapter 7, "Identification") in Seminar XI, for example. *Sex and Gender*[*: The Development of Masculinity and Femininity*] by Robert J. Stoller was published in New York by Science House in 1968 [and London: Hogarth Press, 1968]. *Passage* *à l'acte* and "acting out"*: these two terms are defined and contrasted in Seminar X. Gracián: see the excellent collection edited by Benito Pelegrin (Paris: Seuil, 2005). Mencius: Lacan was familiar with *Mencius on the Mind* by Richards, to which he explicitly refers in Chapter IV of this Seminar.

Class III. The author of the article that angered Lacan was the linguist Georges Mounin, who was a student of André Martinet's; Martinet proposed the theory of "double articulation" that Lacan makes fun of here; see, in Seminar XVI, how Lacan commented on the article when it first came out. Richard Nixon was President of the United States at the time. Houphouët-Boigny was President of Ivory Coast at the time.

Class IV. *The Meaning of Meaning*: Lacan frequently refers to this book (see, for example, *Autres Écrits*, p. 553), which was published, like *Mencius on the Mind*, by Routledge and Kegan Paul. "The Direction of the Treatment and the Principles of Its Power": an article from 1958 that is included in *Écrits*. Starting in Seminar IX, Lacan frequently refers to Peirce's schema. *Éden, Éden, Éden*: a book by Pierre Guyotat which came out in 1971, with prefaces by Leiris, Barthes, and Sollers; the Ministry of the Interior prohibited it from being displayed, advertised, or sold to minors. "The Freudian Thing": an article dating back to 1956, which is included in *Écrits*. Paul Lorenzen's *Métamathématique* came out in 1967.

Class V. The formulation "Eat your *Dasein*" can be found in the "Seminar on 'The Purloined Letter'" on page 29 of *Écrits*; Lacan cited it several times. "Logocentrism" and "arche-writing": terms proffered by the philosopher Jacques Derrida. James Février was the author of the famous *Histoire de l'écriture* [Paris: Payot, 1959]. François Jacob: biologist, Nobel Prize winner, and author of *La Logique du vivant* (Paris: Gallimard, 1970) [*The Logic of Life* (Princeton, NJ: Princeton University Press, 1973], for example. The page in *Écrits* where man's desire is written as Φ(*a*): p. 572. "The Instance of the Letter in the Unconscious": published in 1957 and included in *Écrits*.

Class VI. The Seminar Lacan gave in 1962–1963 is entitled *Identification*.

Class VII. The text entitled "*Lituraterre*" is the first article included in *Autres Écrits*. Lacan's lecture in Bordeaux was published in the collection entitled *My Teaching*, being the third in the series of "Lacan's Paradoxes." Lacan frequently refers to Jacob von Uexküll and to the *Umwelt-Innenwelt* couple. Freud's *Wunderblock* was commented on, in particular, by Jacques Derrida. Freud's letter 52 to Fliess is very often mentioned by Lacan. Frege is discussed in Seminars IX and XII, and at greater length in Seminar XIX. Giuseppe Peano provided, in 1889, a completely axiomatic definition of the set of natural whole numbers, which has since been known as "Peano's arithmetic." "*Sous le pont Mirabeau coule la Seine*" is a line from the poet Apollinaire. The "ear bridge," borrowed from Horus Apollo, can be found on the cover of the journal *La Psychanalyse* (seven issues were published). The *Empire of Signs* was published in French by Skira in 1970 [New York: Hill and Wang, 1982]; it can be found in the excellent edition of Barthes' complete works edited by Éric Marty (Paris: Seuil).

Class VIII. Augustus de Morgan invented and defined "mathematical induction"; Lacan refers to him in Seminar XIV, for one. George Boole worked at, among other things, reducing logic to an algebra. The two mathematicians lived in the first half of the nineteenth century.

Class IX. "The Signification of the Phallus" is included in *Écrits*. "The eternal silence of infinite spaces frightens me": a quote from Pascal's *Pensées*. The *Manava-Dharma-Shastra*, or Book of the Law of Manu, came out in French in the collection of "Classiques Garnier" in March 1939 [first edition 1830], translated from the Sanskrit by Auguste-Louis-Armand Loiseleur-Deslongchamps.

Class X. *Über Sinn und Bedeutung* by Gottlob Frege dates back to 1892. The example including Sir Walter Scott and *Waverley* is Bertrand Russell's, in his epochal article "On Denoting" published in 1905. Rudolf Carnap took up the topic of *Bedeutung* above all in his book *Meaning and Necessity*, published by University of Chicago Press (1947 and 1956). "On a Question Prior to any Possible Treatment of Psychosis": included in *Écrits*. On Sellin, see Seminar XVII.

Index